T0333958

A VERY SHORT,
FAIRLY INTERESTING AND
REASONABLY CHEAP BOOK ABOUT

INTERNATIONAL MARKETING

Also in this series:

A VERY SHORT,
FAIRLY INTERESTING AND
REASONABLY CHEAP BOOK ABOUT

INTERNATIONAL
MARKETING

AJ EARLEY

Los Angeles | London | New Delhi
Singapore | Washington DC | Melbourne

Los Angeles | London | New Delhi
Singapore | Washington DC | Melbourne

SAGE Publications Ltd
1 Oliver's Yard
55 City Road
London EC1Y 1SP

SAGE Publications Inc.
2455 Teller Road
Thousand Oaks, California 91320

SAGE Publications India Pvt Ltd
B 1/I 1 Mohan Cooperative Industrial Area
Mathura Road
New Delhi 110 044

SAGE Publications Asia-Pacific Pte Ltd
3 Church Street
#10-04 Samsung Hub
Singapore 049483

Editor: Matthew Waters
Editorial assistant: Jasleen Kaur
Production editor: Martin Fox
Marketing manager: Lucia Sweet
Cover design: Wendy Scott
Typeset by: C&M Digitals (P) Ltd, Chennai, India
Printed in the UK

The title for the 'A Very Short, Fairly Interesting
and Reasonably Cheap Book about...Series' was
devised by Chris Grey. His book, *A Very Short, Fairly
Interesting and Reasonably Cheap Book about
Studying Organizations*, was the founding title of this
series. Chris Grey asserts his right to be recognized
as founding editor of the A Very Short, Fairly
Interesting and Reasonably Cheap Book about...
Series.

Library of Congress Control Number: 2019935707

British Library Cataloguing in Publication data

A catalogue record for this book is available from the
British Library

ISBN 978-1-5264-5686-1
ISBN 978-1-5264-5687-8 (pbk)

At SAGE we take sustainability seriously. Most of our products are printed in the UK using responsibly
sourced papers and boards. When we print overseas we ensure sustainable papers are used as measured by
the PREPS grading system. We undertake an annual audit to monitor our sustainability.

Contents

Preface

Why This Book is Different

This text will provide you with a much-needed reconsideration of the oft-oversimplified subject of international marketing. It's exciting work, and I'm glad you're giving it a shot.

Before we jump in, however, I need you to take a moment to consider your existing knowledge of the subject. Regardless of the nature of your experience, take some time to think about what themes and topics you associate with international marketing. If you've worked in the field, consider your professional experience. If you have only taken classes, think back to the books you read – you may even flip through the pages of any you still own. For those who are just now engaging seriously with the subject for the first time, consider what you've heard from news reports and media representations. Go on – summarise what you think about international marketing below… be it good, bad, or ugly.

What I currently know about international marketing:

....

....

....

....

....

....

....

....

....

....

....

....

....

Now, I'm going to ask you to take a step back, and think more *abstractly*. Look at your answers above, and even return to texts and sources. Where you've seen international marketing discussed previously, were there common themes, approaches or topics?

Common ways I have seen international marketing represented:

....

....

....

....

....

....

....

....

....

....

....

....

....

....

And finally, one last subject to consider. Do these approaches, narratives, and themes explain everything you wanted to know about international marketing? In past reading, classes, or conversations, did you feel that all the topics that interested you were covered? What you've learned in the past... was it convincing? Write your thoughts on these matters here.

How helpful and explanatory past information is:

....

....

....
....
....
....
....
....
....
....
....
....
....
....

Now, you may be wondering why I'm asking you about such basic things. Put simply, these are the questions that inspired me to write this book that you are reading, at this very moment!

You see, many years ago – in the dark ages even – I was unexpectedly assigned to teach international marketing. It made no sense, as I was arguably better trained to teach almost any other form of marketing – be it strategy, theory, or consumer behaviour. At first, I was gutted. Teaching international marketing is almost considered to be a punishment within certain marketing lecturer circles. I felt I likely received the assignment because I came mid-year, and it was the class no one wanted. All of this may be shocking to you as a reader, as I assume you are keen to learn more about the subject.

I am actually with you on this. International marketing, as a set of business practices, is a fascinating topic. The problem is that much of the past literature on international marketing is not so captivating. It frequently has made an interesting, complex area of human life dull. Even worse, it often fails to explain what it is meant to explain! It is for this reason that I began my work on the subject by considering the very questions listed above. I pored through the existing literature, questioning what it *did* say and what it *did not* say. From there, I started to question *why*. How did it transpire that this field should be so unloved?

The best answer I encountered is that the discipline of international marketing is a 'trickle down of a trickle down'. The argument is that people who work in economics and psychology are 'real researchers', working in 'real fields'. Marketing has stolen much of what it knows from those sorts of scholars (Ellis et al., 2011; Shaw and Jones, 2005), and international marketing is often an afterthought *of marketing itself* – hence 'trickle down of a trickle down'. It is often the case that scholars simply 'tack on' the international bit. They affix it to traditional marketing concepts, which themselves are bastardised versions of ideas from other fields. Yikes!

Still, I felt that there *must* be enough decent published material in the field of international marketing to discuss in a term's worth of lectures. In beginning my course preparations, international marketing appeared to be a dauntingly huge, incorrigible subject. 'Trickle down' of a 'trickle down' caveat aside, scholars and practitioners have claimed that there is a near-infinitude of concepts within this area of marketing practice, and matters only become more complicated once we consider the myriad contexts in which they have done their investigations.

In time, I found that there were actually not that many topics underneath it all! This is both a good and a bad thing. On the negative side, international marketing thought has often left out important phenomena. We see that most of the theories were designed with the largest international corporations in mind, and implications for other types of firms aren't clear. In a world of start-ups and social enterprises, the emphasis on traditional multinationals seemed to describe a bygone era. Indeed, many contemporary social transformations cannot be explained by the outdated theories that grace the pages of our traditional texts. Finally, the field's 'trickle down of a trickle down' nature means that we are left with many applied concepts, but little abstract 'glue' with which to produce a sensible whole.

Interpreting this last matter in a more *positive* light, one could say that there are in fact delightfully few major issues in international marketing. Indeed, I find that most of our existing ideas – *and* important phenomena we have missed – could actually be explained by a handful of principles. All I had to do was go back to materials and methods from 'proper' academic disciplines, and reconsider how everything was connected. Simple! Okay, maybe not so simple. But still, I worked to create a genuine foundation for international marketing, specifically tailored to its own distinctive nature.

I began with a list of key phenomena that we would *want* to understand. I considered not only giant multinationals, but also all potential forms of international business. Here, and throughout this text, I consider cases from small and medium sized enterprises, family-owned business, and in typical (though under-investigated) areas such as logistics. Then, I considered what disciplines could actually explain these matters. I found that the parent disciplines of economics and psychology weren't always a great fit for the phenomena of interest. At their worst, they seemed to obscure (rather than clarify) the main controversies and contestations of this domain of business practice. I actually had to look to fields such as history, politics, ethical philosophy, development studies and even media studies *as well as* the usual suspects (economics, psychology, and sometimes anthropology) to explain what is specifically different about international practice. This text is the culmination of that work.

The Introduction which follows will present my new framework. For now, there are a few things you should know about my style as a researcher and educator. These will help you to make sense of this book.

To begin, I follow a **Socratic approach** to liberal education. The 'Socratic' part is just an unfortunate academic way of saying that I believe in building knowledge from where people are at. I think that all sorts of people can come up with very sophisticated answers to the most complex questions of our day. Philosophy doesn't have to be something relegated to ivory towers – as noted by anthropologist David Graeber (2013), most human societies are debating the big questions about society, life, and government all the time. Taking this sort of *self-referential* approach to your study will also help you learn more effectively, and more easily make connections to your own life. Taken together, I like to think of myself as a facilitator of learning, more than a teacher.

The 'liberal' bit means that I believe that big topics from a wide range of disciplines are worth knowing, even if you aren't going to do a full degree in any of those programmes. Over the course of the book, I will teach you bits about not only history, ethics, and politics, but also anthropology, sociology, media studies, and even climate science. Liberal education philosophies contend that knowing a little something about everything helps everyone in everyday life. Here, I take inspiration from Aronowitz (2001). Aronowitz argues that higher education tends to be stymied by its lack of interest in the real world, but also that philosophy is of such universal value that it should be taught in working class, vocational and 'trade' curricula.

All said, while I allow you to teach yourself wherever I can, there are places where it is helpful for me to 'teach' things I have learned – what is called 'didactic' practice. While self-guided education is great, and done in a slow, intensive, one-on-one way could be used to make many people expert in many things, sometimes it does help to 'fast forward' and tell you about things that I have learned myself. Often, this material was gleaned from a huge range of academic sources, so... thank me later, for saving you the work of having to read all of that yourself!

Ultimately, I am interested in the development of systematic knowledge. This is generally considered to be the goal of all **theory development** – not only to describe different phenomena, but also to connect them to one another and also to conditions (matters of what, when, why, and how). This also involves abstraction, even to the level of philosophical concepts, based on the idea that very abstract notions can be used in a wide range of situations.

This is particularly crucial in the case of international marketing, as the discipline has often treated firms and their figureheads as isolated actors, working as if no one and nothing were constraining their actions. Here, we see that international marketing practice is actually highly *interdependent* and *contingent* – determined by not only a wide range of business principles, but by what others are doing as well.

Again, while the problem with past international marketing texts is that they were too short on explanations, that doesn't mean the solution is hundreds of new theories. Good theory development is actually based on **parsimony** – the identification of a handful of very effective, very explanatory tools to help us understand the world.

In time, I find a rigorous, scholarly approach to international marketing is valuable not only in its own right, but also as it raises questions which marketing and even various parent disciplines should consider too!

So… sit back… relax… and prepare to rethink everything you know about international marketing!

Introduction

What is International Marketing, Really?

When I first started tearing through traditional international marketing texts, I couldn't shake the feeling that the authors were talking about something different than what they were nominally talking about. They would mention the name of a firm like Apple or Google, but wouldn't explain what type of firms they were. It was then unclear what type of strategies they were using. For an academic like myself, who specialises in the study of language, this is a big red flag. When authors seem to be talking about something else subtextually, it's a sign to keep digging.

What I found was that international marketing tended to be defined in practice by a single business model – that of the 'Glorious Global Brand', as I describe it. This introduction presents that finding, critiques the model, and then brings you an alternative perspective. It also lays out a roadmap of the rest of the book, which explores this new approach in greater detail.

Identifying and Critiquing the 'Glorious Global Brand'

Most key texts start from a fair, broad definition of international marketing – like '*all marketing occurring across national borders*'. Unfortunately, that's not what they actually discuss or study. Throughout the course of such texts, I noticed that 'best practice' in international marketing is often defined by a very limited constellation of strategies, which work best for only a few types of organisation. This is the model of the large, publicly traded, almost-always-American, multinational corporation.

There is not only little consideration of what falls outside of this remit – but also little synthesis concerning what is studied *within* the remit. Here, I asked, what is it that is so valuable about this one model? What is being endorsed? In other words, I looked at how the authors characterised these firms.

These organisations are often portrayed as caring companies – excelling in customer-orientation and engaging in highly publicised corporate social responsibility programmes. Most examples come from B2C – business-to-consumer – firms, often neglecting the work that they and B2B – business-to-business – firms do with many smaller partners. Where 'product industries' are concerned, we see an emphasis on the marketing labour done, and little consideration of how this relates to the production labour that goes into the products. In other words, 'value creation' is seen to be something that happens in advertising firms, not factories. While it is undeniable that this is one major model of international marketing practice which is actually performed throughout the world (Apple and Google *are* real!), this is an insufficient foundation for work which is supposedly about 'all marketing across national borders'. I explain the reasons why here.

First, while Glorious Global Brands do account for a significant amount of global economic activity, there is so much which occurs outside of this envelope. Indeed, there arguably are only a handful of firms for which this model is appropriate. A huge (and arguably larger) percentage of international marketing activity is conducted through small and medium sized enterprises (SMEs); in B2B contexts; and by those operating in more peripheral locations, rather than global centres. The setting is nearly always the Global North, with the Global South represented as a new set of markets for the former to seize upon. The international marketing environment also raises questions about traditional financial models, and as such development-based and fair trade models should be of particular interest to international marketing scholars… otherwise, where will they be studied? Put simply, I believe it is of great value for practitioners and students alike to think of their future employment beyond that of the Glorious Global Brands, as greater opportunities for advancement, earning, and profit are often available through other sorts of enterprises. Indeed, the main attractions of the model – huge margins (and executive take-home pay) based on tremendous economies of scale that only one or two global leaders have access to – are by definition only accessible to a small percentage of marketing practitioners.

Second, strategies developed from the Glorious Global Brands model only have limited applicability in real life international marketing contexts. As noted by de Mooij (2019) and Usunier and Lee (2013), who have their own pioneering critiques of this model, these strategies have developed primarily from a single corner of American business practice. As such, their applicability to other cultures is often limited. Given that we are generally dealing with intercultural considerations as much as we are dealing with international ones, this is a BIG limitation!

A third critique, from my own study, is that the focus on the 'sexy', customer-focused parts of international marketing (like advertising) leaves students and practitioners ill-prepared for much of the actual, profit-making work of international marketing. I find that the majority of the value is produced by what currently occupies the unsexy 'back of the book' pages. Relevant strategies include gaining control over pricing structures; effectively managing distribution channels; specialising in distribution (either logistics or retailing); conducting business-to-business dealings internationally; and growing business via mergers and acquisitions.

The fourth reason is that new economic sectors have emerged, which are not well integrated into these texts, and not well served by the theories therein. Particularly relevant are changes within services marketing, especially the rise of new web-mediated services. Textbooks and research have mostly only caught up with the 'first wave' of services marketing, occurring in traditional sectors such as hospitality and food service. In time, however, entirely unforeseen services have emerged and become quite central to the economy. Relevant firms include information and advertising servicers such as Google; social media platforms like Facebook; apps, which simultaneously provide value and harvest data; streaming services like iTunes, YouTube, and Spotify, which provide value by aggregating licensed content in exchange for cash or watching adverts; and online retailers like Amazon, which obliterate the model of their bricks-and-mortar forefathers. In cases like these, the marketing practices are a part of the value creation itself.

Starting from these critiques, I had my work set out for me! I set out to develop new conceptual tools to understand these pressing issues—all while ensuring that more traditional contexts could still be explained! In so doing, I also had to be mindful of whether new business practices were actually as new as they seemed. I often do find that much of the supposed 'new economy' can be viewed as the old in new packaging – as marketing markets itself to *seem* more current or benevolent than it often is.

I present my perspective next. I argue that the diversity of international marketing practice can be easily explained through a handful of principles. The full list is summarised in the Appendix, but I will provide a brief taster here.

Envisioning an Alternative: New Principles of International Marketing

My approach is based on the fact that there are three disciplines which are *particularly* relevant for understanding international marketing, but which have not been well-integrated (as economics and psychology have, for example). These are the fields of history, ethics and politics. I begin with history in Chapter 1, as this shows what international marketing has been constructed as over time. My first 'new' principle is that the composition, dynamics, and practices of contemporary international marketing are largely shaped by historical relationships and processes. Here, I dig deeper into matters such as the perceived superiority of the American MNC model. Ultimately, we need to go much further back, to the (often colonialist) European origins of modern, industrial-era international marketing practice.

Chapter 2 meanwhile draws on the discipline of ethics proper – not just business ethics – as I elucidate the ethical dimensions of international marketing practice. This chapter can be summarised by the principle that the ethical stakes of international marketing are often hidden, complicated, and difficult to impact – but they are nevertheless tremendous. Here, questions about the impact of powerful commercial actors within society and government naturally arise. As discussions of 'power' are just shorthand for discussions of 'politics', I turn to this discipline next in Chapter 3. I argue that international marketing is inherently political, as politics are the exercise of power. As such, I argue that we need to make better use of political analysis, as it can provide superior insight into the nature and dynamics of more specific marketing environments, as well as into the viability of various marketing strategies.

Part II is titled Rethinking Practices, and it begins the work of translating these big theoretical considerations into concrete, applicable knowledge. Chapter 4 is dedicated to marketing management, reconsidering it in terms of both these new foundations *and* the true diversity of firms and strategies. Here I critically interrogate traditional notions of what drives internationalisation (and potential profitability from it). Chapter 5 then looks specifically at consumer issues. Rather than rehashing standard material from the field of consumer behaviour, I focus on how consumer culture has historically been engineered to maximise value production. This involves convincing people to think of themselves as consumers, rather than as workers or citizens. Chapter 6 takes these matters even further, considering what can be learned from intercultural marketing. Here, we investigate the derivation of value from culture including appropriation, hybridisation, and cultural imperialism.

Throughout Part II, traditional market relations are recast via this perspective. Here, we see that the sort of sensitive, nuanced market research which occurs in developed contexts is not practised equally throughout the world. Indeed, many firms avoid doing this work by seeking political (brute force) strategies such as establishing de facto monopolies, rather than winning customers by consent. Big brands win through aggressive distribution and integration of their goods and services to the point that consumers do not consider any alternative. How many of us, for example, use a search engine that isn't Google? All of this ultimately raises questions about traditional models of business and consumer ethics.

While Part I looked to the past and Part II seeks to make sense of the present, Part III looks to the future. Here, I argue that the biggest developments in international marketing since it was originally theorised are the emergence of new media, and the inevitability of climate change. In Chapter 7, I begin by briefly clarifying what is truly 'new' (and not new) about new media, and then work to elucidate what is truly valuable about new media for international marketing. The key takeaway here is that while new media have certain benefits (e.g. decreasing the cost and timeline of international communications), many of the same principles of marketing and communications apply to these media as well.

Chapter 8 does not simply provide a 'sustainability component', but instead theorises how (un)sustainability is part and parcel of standard international marketing practice. The guiding truism here is that international marketing is logically (and practically) more carbon-intensive. Think about it – stereotypical 'Glorious Global Brands' are those with one centre, and which distribute products *all over the world*. It is as if the model was produced to *maximise* the carbon footprint of commerce! Looking to history, we see that this is the intent, as it does produce the greatest value for very small sets of very powerful stakeholders. As unsustainability is built into the system (see, for example, 'planned obsolescence'), the challenge of climate change potentially makes international marketing a doomsday machine. At the same time, current climate science indicates that we can no longer ignore the negative impacts. Here, I draw upon the knowledge of history and politics we developed in earlier chapters to produce some insight into what the 'end game' of climate change is likely to be, given that the Glorious Multinationals are unlikely to change their strategies under current conditions.

The book concludes by attempting to reassemble international marketing, after the critiques levied in the preceding chapters. From a straightforward, practical perspective, it explains how international marketing is likely to continue into the future, and how individual marketers can understand their practice better with an adequate understanding of its historical and political foundations. Based upon my general principles, it makes clear the possibilities and potentials within any set of marketing conditions. I also use the conclusion to bring together the ethical considerations raised throughout – with questions which emerge from histories of colonialism, imperialism, and artificially manufactured unequal trade relations. Here, it is important to acknowledge that for many workers, there are no options within current strictures – they have little actual opportunity to engage in genuine ethical deliberation or activity. As such, the focus is on critiquing those who *do* operate the controls of the machine, as they largely dictate the terms by which the rest of us operate.

PART I

New Foundations

As noted in the Introduction, this Part introduces three additional disciplines which I find are necessary to truly understand international marketing practice: that of history, ethics, and politics. Here, I will provide a very brief note on why these disciplines are important; how they come together; and a bit more detail on what will happen in each chapter.

Following notions of liberal education, it is best to have a foundation that spans the entirety of academic traditions. As we already have learned much from economics, psychology, anthropology, and cultural studies, my project is to identify the most urgent elisions. At a basic level, one could argue for greater integration of history, ethics and politics simply because they are three *huge* areas of social research which have historically been ignored within marketing thought. In practice, I also find that these three 'missing' foundations often tell us *more* about international marketing than many of the parent disciplines with which we usually associate!

Before jumping in, I should give you a preview of how these three disciplines will come together. To start, we must acknowledge that there are big differences between these three subjects. Each one is an entire academic discipline, and people get PhDs in all of them! Each discipline also brings with it particular methods, which are better-suited for some phenomena, and ill-suited for others. In introducing this material, I try to keep the disciplines as separate as possible, and I try to use cases which are clearly best-explained by one of the three disciplines.

All said, it should be acknowledged that even here, many cases can be fruitfully explored via history, ethics or politics. You may want to explore the multifaceted nature of cases further in your own time. To get some sense of how to do this, I recommend examining later chapters (in Parts II and III), where I allow for more of the natural overlap in disciplines to return.

Through the chapters presented here, it is my hope that you will now have a better sense of not only the concepts from these three areas, but their methods. This is because the different methods used by each will allow you to make different sorts of *arguments*. Historical arguments can be used to show that practice has not been the same at all times, and in all places. It can be used to think proactively about what the future might be like, given what we know about similar situations or human life more generally. Ethical arguments, meanwhile, are grounded in very abstract principles about 'right and wrong'. In other words, you should be able to explain your actions in any given situation based on principles which guide your life. Political arguments, meanwhile, concern the viability of various options based on resources and power within a given situation. In achieving any gains in your life, be they business or personal, you must have a realistic understanding of what you can accomplish, and what those in competition with you are trying to achieve. In cases where power is great, responsibility is also great, which means that there is a large amount of ethical burden upon any choice made.

Ultimately, the best approach is one which remains open to the potential of a variety of perspectives, but which can be flexible and decisive when one foundation is of greater use in explaining a particular matter.

I introduce history first, not because I think it can more easily be understood without recourse to the other two disciplines, but because looking at history can provide us with a useful new definition of international marketing based on the historical formations which have produced it, and on accumulated evidence about what international marketing tends to be, in practice. The second chapter, on ethics, presents principles which can guide our actions within this historically determined and politically charged domain of social activity. The third chapter builds upon this, showing how politics gives us language to give a further, deeper definition of what these practices are.

1

Historical Emergence

This chapter presents a history of international marketing practice. The hope that we can understand what international marketing is, before we start making pronouncements about how it should be done (ethics) and how it works in practice (via political analysis).

While most of us will have been subjected to a great number of history classes in our lifetimes, the basic details of what history *is* are often skipped over, so I will start the chapter by properly introducing what this discipline does. Here, I start from Howell and Prevenier's (2001) guidance, and cite further references where appropriate. Don't worry, I won't be asking you to write a complete history of the world at the end of this text... the point here is to introduce *just* enough of the theory and method to understand how histories are produced. You can then feel more confident in reading, interpreting and using historical arguments in your day-to-day life.

Next, the chapter presents a chronological explanation of the emergence and spread of international marketing. Here I begin by identifying the ancient origins of international marketing, before moving on to the forms international marketing has taken under mercantilism, early modern capitalism, 20th century global capitalism, and contemporary neoliberalism. Building on the work of Tosh (2009, 2008), I argue that reading histories is valuable not only for documenting *what has happened*, but also for helping us understand ourselves and *what the future is likely to hold*. As the old saying goes... those who do not learn from history are doomed to repeat it! Throughout, the principle of international marketing at play is the following:

Principle 1: The composition, dynamics, and practices of contemporary international marketing are largely shaped by historical relationships and processes.

What Is History?

History sits in an awkward position between the arts and social sciences. While many initially think that history is objective, especially where we see evidence such as direct quotes, it is also an undeniably creative endeavour. With this paradox in mind, critical historiographers provide the best definition of what history *really* is. They define the **historical method** as the production of **narratives** (stories) about events, people, and societies (MacMillan, 2010; Gunn, 2006). It is often found that the stories can be quite inaccurate or biased. While this may seem like it would undermine the potential value of a narrative, this is often what historians are interested in – the ways in which stories are told from particular, invested perspectives. Understanding the meaning of any story requires **critical reading** practice, taking into account the motivations of the author, and the wider historical context. Here, we should also engage in **reflexive practice** (awareness of our own potential biases).

Of course, there are cases where producing the 'best possible' or 'most complete' account is desired – rather than simply engaging in a critical reading of any story. Historians have methods to improve **rigour** (in other words, to engage in the best possible evidence gathering). More scientific approaches to history begin with a portrait of what the ideal accounts would be (e.g. the stories of *all* participants at an event), and then work to find the best available subset from that. For some phenomena, there may only be a single individual witness or survivor, which raises questions about **corroboration** (as there is no one else to confirm what happened). Here we see the value of critical reading once again, as historians collect and analyse evidence about the source and his/her reliability, as well as the socio-historic context. As noted by Ginzburg (1999), the ultimate goal is to better understand the world around us through practices of meaning-making, contextualisation, and theorisation. Here, we should be concerned with relevance as well as verifiability.

The major traditions within history are defined by the types of phenomena they investigate. Claus and Marriott (2012) provide a very valuable introduction to the various types, complete with examples of particularly well-conceived histories, if you are interested in considering the topic further. Here, I will focus on discussing a few types of history which can be relevant to the study of international marketing. To begin, **social histories** focus on societies, while **political histories** examine political moments, movements and/or governments. **Economic histories** show how economic systems came to be. **Cultural histories** examine how a culture changed over time, and may draw on anthropological methods and evidence as well as that from history. **Visual histories** study changing conventions of visual representation. **People's histories** try to describe events from the vantage point of an average observer (rather than an elite), while **feminist histories** are interested in the role of gender during historical events. **Postcolonial** approaches to history shine light upon the struggle of nations for self-determination (Gunn, 2006).

Throughout this text, I rely primarily on **global histories**, which do just what they say... they examine how historical phenomena are parts of larger, even global social processes. Many different scholars are known for some sort of **world systems** approach, and I refer to several throughout the chapter. Chronological sections map roughly onto the work of Samir Amin (2014 [1997]). Elsewhere, Wallerstein's (2004) world systems approach is key, as it examines how an interlocking economic system has emerged. A postcolonial perspective is also brought into the fold, as it is an important counterpoint to the traditional global histories. This approach is likely to be a bit different from those of previous histories you have read, given that it emphasises complex processes that are long in the making, rather than discrete events (as with traditional chronologies).

At the same time, the goals of this chapter require me to consider social, political, economic, and business histories as well. Here, we will take a more dispassionate look at how international marketing practice emerged, which often requires problematising the past conduct of powerful nations. While some may question this move, it is absolutely essential for producing a realistic portrait of what international marketing actually is. Indeed, doing anything else prevents small firms, and those from small nations, from understanding the challenges they face in international market entry.

The 'Why' of International Marketing: Origins and Motivations

Trade has crossed cultural and/or national borders for thousands of years, and as such, international marketing practice is much older than we might think. The benevolent narrative often espoused in international marketing texts is that trade emerged because tribes, cultures, and nation-states had different abilities and resources, and as such everyone benefitted from exchanging what they could produce easily for rare goods from others. This was undoubtedly true in early, incomplete economies, and for those who lived in inhospitable climates. But questions remained about why trade would flourish elsewhere...

What about the case of more evenly matched societies, with fairly complete economies? Why would they engage in

international trade? What would the point be? Take a minute to think about these questions below. Note: the answer is not (just) profit... how would profit be made?

....

....

....

....

....

....

....

....

....

....

....

....

....

....

In examining the real motivations for international commerce, it is helpful to start with Walby's (2009) accounts of the evolution of economic systems, from ancient times to the present. Here, we find that benevolence tends to be a motivation in the earliest of international commerce, but starts to fade even in ancient civilisations. Increasingly, we see a handful of governments with disproportionate power, who use this in order to gain trade advantages over other countries. Other potential motivations, such as **novelty**, are comparatively small and account for a small amount of international marketing to this day. And benevolence, to those who live in inhospitable climates? Forget even that! Increasingly, we take advantage of the disadvantages of other societies, rather than seeking to 'lift each other up'.

What's more, historical research on early consumer culture tells us much about the real foundations of international business systems. As noted by Rassuli and Hollander (1986: 5), each of the first big, ancient economies – China, India, Egypt, Sumeria, Assyria, Persia, and Babylonia – emerged alongside imperial socio-economic structures. These are forms of statecraft that brought military and diplomatic force together with business, in order to ensure favourable trading terms for the imperial power. So favourable in fact that early examples of mass consumer cultures could be found at the imperial centres of these trading systems... though much less so in the peripheries of them. Interesting...

In this world of real limits to resources and labour, abundant material wealth tends to exist when a power (or several powers) has the ability to accumulate a disproportionately high amount of material goods and (from ancient Egypt onwards) money. The forms of domination under-girding such systems have varied over time, from the intentionally confusing use of authority (e.g. the use of banking as an explanation for unequal trade) to outright theft and enslavement. Zak Cope (2015) is quick to note that while the former seems *comparatively* benign, its effects can be equally insidious, as material deprivation of weaker trading partners leads to poverty and often death. The only difference is that... people don't know why they died. And of course, we all know much about the horrors of international business over time... but do we know all the details? Cope finds that contemporary notions of race were largely developed to justify economic divisions of labour such as slavery. In reality, there is no legitimate foundation of racial categories, and there could be any set of categorisations imaginable (or none!).

Trade continued and developed from ancient times to the present. Nation-states became increasingly wealthy, as did individual business owners, and both products and processes became more sophisticated. New eras of high economic activity were seen in the cases of the Ottoman Empire (1299–1922), China's Ming Dynasty (1368–1644), and Japan's Tokugawa era (1603–1868). A new blueprint for international commerce emerged with **mercantilisim** in Europe. This is an approach where countries strived to be the most powerful **exporter** of particular goods, because exporting maintains the value of goods domestically, and produces valuable tax revenue for governments. **Protectionist** economic policies, produced with the hopes of taxing trade partners more than one was taxed, were a common feature. Successful mercantilist governments could use their proceeds to gain further control of weaker countries via military, diplomatic, and business conquest. That said, as a successful mercantilist government was so valuable, power contests *within* regions and nations were also quite common.

As noted by Kotler and Levy (1969), marketing refers to the processes of bringing goods, services, or ideas to market, by either for-profit or non-profit entities. International marketing is that which occurs across international or intercultural boundaries (Baack et al.,

2018). From this look into the early history of international marketing practice, we see that it was rarely motivated by benevolence. The message to take forward in the rest of this chapter, and the rest of the book, is two-fold. First, the same notion that 'what's seen as fair is fair' persists to this day, and is arguably the logic of international marketing. Second, allowing this logic to run unchecked for thousands of years has created a world economy defined by huge inequalities. While some countries struggle for subsistence, others have far more than they need (at least on a per capita basis – of course, most developed countries still have internal poverty, which I will discuss more later). Many see this as acceptable given that the initial acts of deception occurred so long ago. Others have sought to naturalise these distinctions, creating stories about why this state of affairs is justifiable or natural.

Again, it is notable that much of the work of creating inequality is ongoing and considered to be quite uncontroversial. At the same time, the effects of these callous actions are real for those living 'on the other side of the equation'. The sections that follow consider the evolution of unequal trade within early modern capitalism, 20th century geopolitics, and the contemporary moment.

The Beginning of Early Modern International Marketing

The foundation of the contemporary world economic system – capitalism – began to emerge in earnest in the 19th century. As noted by historian Nikolai Bukharin (1987 [1929]), this period is characterised by a transition from the stiff protectionism of mercantilism to increasing cross-border cooperation – at least in cases where it would lead to superior economic productivity for both nations. At this moment, we see the rise of modern **finance**, where lending was increasingly seen as an end in itself. Cross-border **investment** began apace in this era. Over time, this produced the **transnational economic systems** and **multinational firms** that are so familiar to us today.

A second key development here is the foundation of what Bukharin calls the **city–countryside divide**. This is a process which is as old as finance, but which accelerated rapidly in the 19th century. As economies developed and technology improved, craftspeople and farmers were increasingly expected to adopt new (often costly) methods so as to stay competitive. This required the sort of funding that was frankly impossible to produce within a traditional village society. Banks offered such finance with interest, growing and growing their capital reserves. In time, financial centres (generally in cities) had **power** over more remote areas, given the concentration of wealth they possessed (see also Wood, 2002). While banks could control interest rates to their advantage, traders and retailers also had power over small producers, as their cooperation was increasingly necessary for survival. In time, this has led to the dramatic differences in wages between country and city that we see in almost every part of the world. In the 19th century, this increasingly became a **global division of labour**, with entire countries increasingly focused on commerce, and others relegated to farming or manufacturing.

Two further strategies that were foundational to early modern capitalism are **colonialism** and **imperialism**. On these topics, I take inspiration from Harvey (2005). The former refers to the full control of one territory by another, which was often nominally defended as 'benevolent', but which we well know has been used to justify historical abuses such as slavery and the exploitation of children as labourers. The latter, meanwhile, refers to cases where the powerful party may not have *complete* control over government, but has tremendous influence over the country's affairs and economy. Often times, the more powerful party demanded the formal sworn allegiance or legally-codified trade partnerships with the weaker parties.

It is notable that powerful nations directly siphoned resources out of weaker ones via colonialism and imperialism. Zak Cope (2015) presents the harrowing case of how India had been developing perfectly well *before* the 'benevolence' of British imperialism. By imposing preferential, unfair trade relations upon India, Great Britain was actually able to amass so much capital that it used these proceeds to finance its industrial revolution. Building on a range of cases such as these, Parenti (2011) argues that gaps in development are largely attributable to **over-exploitation** rather than underdevelopment:

> From ancient eras to more recent centuries [the nations of the periphery] had produced magnificent civilizations capable of impressive feats in architecture, horticulture, irrigation, arts, crafts, medicines, public hygiene, and the like, superior in many respects to what was found among the ill-washed, priest-ridden diseased populations of European Christendom. Quite frequently it was contact with the western colonizers that brought poverty and disaster to the indigenous populations of Africa, Latin America, and elsewhere. Once their farmlands and crops were stolen, their resources plundered, their herds slaughtered, their townships destroyed, their people enslaved, deep poverty was the inescapable outcome, leaving them to be denounced as lazy, backward, and

stupid. In fact, they were not underdeveloped but overexploited. Their development was never allowed to proceed in peace and self-direction. (Parenti, 2011: 51)

At the end of the day, there is no inherent justification for why these wage disparities should exist – they simply do because powerful actors decided they should, in their own interests. Given these facts, colonial and imperial arrangements are retrospectively considered to be quite deceptive and unethical. At the same time, there has never been an adequate recalibration of the world economy to ameliorate these issues. The global division of labour wrought by imperialism and colonialism has actually become foundational to 20th century and contemporary economic systems. For example, we still see significantly elevated levels of commerce between the United Kingdom and its former colonies. We also see widespread wealth inequality between colonisers and colonised, that persists to the present.

Overproduction in Early Industrial, Colonial, and Imperial Economies

The Industrial Revolution, which had begun in earnest in the 18th century but reached its truly revolutionary potential in the 19th century, brought with it dramatic changes to economies. These changes had particularly stark effects on countries which lagged even a tiny bit in the race towards automation. This was exacerbated, rather than eased, by colonial and imperial relationships. Rather than caring for the countries under their umbrellas, the marginally more developed countries leading such relationships actually harmed the weaker countries in a variety of ways, to support their own domestic productivity. I explain these histories below.

To begin, the industrial revolution triggered a **crisis of overproduction**. Put simply, the majority of consumers even in developed countries could not mop up the increased flow of goods available with mechanical production. These were societies where individuals might have been accustomed to getting a new blanket every two years, from their neighbour, in exchange for a steady supply of eggs. While there were certainly some benefits and conveniences from higher supply, demand could not meet what could now be produced. This is largely attributable to principles which governed the **distribution of wealth.** While each industrial enterprise would have benefitted from higher consumption, each had no incentive to pay workers well, so factory workers (as well as peasants) had little to spend in this economy. This sort of vicious cycle persists to the present day, and is unfortunate as it actually suppresses economies.

What imperial powers managed to do was **dump** (yes, that's the proper term!) massive amounts of cheaply produced products onto their colonial dependents. You might think this would have led to a great improvement in quality of life, but that was not the case. There are three reasons for this.

First, while these goods were cheap, they were not provided for nothing. Obtaining them meant active participation in imperial and colonial trade networks, in exchange for currency accepted by traders. This generally involved doing work that was undesirable and often not even appropriate for local conditions. One of the main formats was through what is known as **commodity monoculture**. This is a sort of agriculture where a region (or even entire country) specialises in one particular product. The choice was historically guided by the wants and needs of empire. Key examples are the world's coffee, chocolate, and sugar producing regions. In some places, this took advantage of local knowledge, but more frequently, it required intensive development of specialised horticultural knowledge with little alternative application.

These systems were furthered by the dumping of agricultural products, which made traditional methods of farming economically unsustainable. This led to a decline in subsistence farming, and complete reliance of dependent countries on more powerful ones for covering their basic needs. In situations of complete control, the terms of exchange (for both goods and labour) were of course terribly exploitative. In one of the worst instances, at United Fruit Company's Latin American operations, labourers were so terribly paid that they engaged in mutiny. Unfortunately for them, they were also so poorly valued that the firm saw no issue in bringing in mercenaries to kill them (Chapman, 2009).

Second, the types of goods dumped often involved little consideration of local needs, as the only marketing standard was the sort of *return* which could be made possible. While one could say that 'people don't buy what they don't want', a variety of cases teach us that this is not always the case. We will discuss this in more detail in Chapter 6, but I will provide one example here. It is derived from Gabrielle Palmer's (2009) work on the marketing of formula milk internationally.

Palmer finds that there was no significant demand for formula milk before the 19th century, as society was structured around breastfeeding, so women generally stayed with their children – or took their children with them wherever they had to go! On rare occasions where this was not possible, social systems like wet-nursing (feeding another woman's child) could be used. As such, 'baby formula' was actually invented simply because there was far too much milk being produced with the advent of mechanical milking. It was crashing markets across Europe, devastating dairy farmers. The solution chosen to save **domestic markets** was to export formula milk both locally and internationally. With absolutely no scientific evidence that formula milk could replace breastmilk, companies such as Nestlé put the product to market and hoped not too many infants would die. In the short run, this proved true, but early unfortified formulas (basically powdered milk, so no more valuable than cow's milk that would have been readily and cheaply available) lacked key nutrients that support cognitive development. The full impact of this downside was only known over the course of decades.

As time went on, the marketing of formula in less-developed countries led to significant increases in infant mortality. One reason for this was that babies could not survive in some contexts without the antibodies from their mothers. Elsewhere, formula was given quite expensive prices, knowing that women who had chosen formula (and thus could no longer lactate) would be dependent on paying at all costs. These women did pay whatever they could, often plunging their families into poverty. In other cases, that income could not be reliably had, so babies died of starvation. Benevolence? I think not...

Third, Bukharin (1987 [1929]) makes the potentially interesting point that the cost of the goods dumped in a weaker territory could be so low as to not be profitable within that territory, as long as it improved the overall economy of scale of the entire business. That may sound shocking, but as you likely know, the concept of **economy of scale** means that the bigger a business is, the cheaper it is to make an individual unit. For example, if I, as a lecturer, were to start making shoes, my first few would be *very* costly! I would have to recoup training and facilities costs. There would be materials, which I would likely be buying in small quantities at the highest margins, and it is quite probable that I would not know the best materials distributors when I started business. I likely wouldn't know what I was doing, and would have a number of discarded pairs that must also be recouped. If I dedicated my life to it, however, and opened a factory employing many trained shoemakers, the cost per pair would go down dramatically. If they went from making 1,000 to 10,000 pairs per year, I could pressure my suppliers to give me the best possible materials prices, under the threat that I would otherwise go elsewhere.

Bukharin noted that there often exists a point where selling more units for no profit (or even a small loss) is valuable, as it brings the cost of production for the entire organisation down so low that margins in other areas are high enough to compensate for it. Complicated, I know, but mathematically (and historically!) true. The consequence is that there was absolutely no basis upon which weaker nations or firms could compete against this sort of model. As you'd imagine, these aspects of dumping tended to obliterate traditional economies. While some could say that this is natural progress, dumping was another tactic whereby countries that were marginally less developed, or simply unwilling to engage in the sorts of commercial warfare employed by more powerful countries, never had the opportunity to reach their best possible productivity levels.

One would think that the proceeds of colonial and imperial capitalism had improved the lives of domestic populations tremendously. Imagine, all those cheap products! This was also not the case. The powerful colonial/imperial nations actually used a variety of tactics grounded in their transnational trade economies to make life *more difficult* for their own citizenry. An excellent case can be found in the work of anthropologist Sidney Mintz (1985), who examined the many purposes that sugar served for powerful nations. As seen above, sugar was produced by a commodity monoculture for maximum profitability. Did they let their own people know this? Not really, as that **information** (factual knowledge of the economic situation) could have been used for consumers' advantage.

In Europe, and especially in Britain, sugar served two purposes. First, it was priced and marketed as cheaper than the equivalent amount of farm produce, so that labour could be freed from agriculture to work in factories. Sugar was used not only as a preservative, which could improve quality of life by making farm food last, but it was increasingly seen as a food replacement. Coffee and tea were also a part of this new diet, as they could stave off hunger. Women were particularly susceptible to being subjected to this menu, as it was argued that their labour (back on the farm and minding perhaps 10 children) was not physical enough to require what little 'real food' remained. Quite shockingly, the UK's largest increase in sugar consumption actually occurred in the 19th not the 20th century (Mintz, 1985). The ill health effects of overconsumption of poor quality food also began in earnest during this time. Sadly, nutrition in undisturbed peasant communities is often superior to that in modern economies.

In time, we reach the second use of sugar. Once domestic consumers were completely dependent, prices were raised, so as to further increase revenue. Sugar was marketed as a luxury, and the desirability of sweets and desserts was heavily promoted. In doing so, sugar became an essential part of diet and economy throughout the developed world, and these economies were manipulated so as to produce the highest possible profit. This was sadly a bitter deal, as time went on. The overall level of food provision fell, and factory wages were rarely adequate for the more luxurious sweets.

So, next time you go to Starbucks, take a moment to think about the origins of the £5 luxury meal in front of you. The combination of sweetened, milky tea or coffee with biscuits or pastries was produced literally because it was the cheapest possible, least nutritious foodstuffs. Even to this day, the ingredients are generally obtained by very unequal trade relationships, and the margins are unbelievably huge. The goal of such a snack is to quickly make one feel full, so work can be resumed. To add insult to injury, this has since been marketed as some sort of luxury with the emergence of artisan lattes and award-winning baristas.

It must also be noted that the proceeds of controlling economic relationships were not returned to dependent nations – much as official narratives in countries like the UK would like us to believe. Looking at historical documents, one can see that the sheer arrogance of colonial powers at the time was astounding. Consider, for instance, the poster

Figure 1.1   Poster from the Empire Marketing Board (1927) revealing the logic of British Imperialism in terms of labour, resources and market-making. National Archive. Fair dealing/used for illustration and education.

from the 'Empire Marketing Board' below (originally published 1927). Here we see the colonies referred to as a source of resources, labour (via 'goods received') and as a market for surplus goods. The African colonies are referred to as a monolithic entity and customers are referred to in terms of sales figures, with no detail or nuance. In another poster from the organisation, decorated with flying Union Jack flags, individuals were implored to 'Be Patriotic: Buy Empire Grown Tea' – as if everything produced within the empire rightfully belonged to British firms (see Rappaport, 2015 for an extended discussion of this shocking campaign). This is further evidence for Cope's (2015) assertion that the colonies were sources of revenue, receiving an inadequate return for their labour.

The 20th Century: Further Development of the World Economy

In the late 19th and early 20th centuries, Amin (2014 [1997]) argues that the structures of the world economy began to formalise and crystallise. While early modern capitalism still had some vestiges of mercantilism, there was increasingly a drive against protectionism, as it was seen to be a game from which there are never sustainable gains. Even if one manages an impressive tariff for some period, this will undoubtedly lead to a trade war, which will negate the results. Interestingly, we are now witnessing a reversal of this thinking back towards economic nationalism, most notably in America under Trump's administration ('America First' and 'Buy American, Hire American').

At the turn of the 20th century, **national power** remained a dominant organising logic, but the supposed basis and justification for it was on specialisation, rather than being momentarily clever in the tariff game. Countries increasingly recognised each other's projects, and unprofitable ventures were often abandoned. At the same time, nationalist movements were arising in colonies throughout the world, and much of the colonial project had to be abandoned. Empire was in swift retreat.

One would think that all was progressing in a cooperative way, despite the fact that the unequal foundations of competition were never addressed, but the World Wars changed all that. Economic rivalries played a significant role in conflicts. Meanwhile, the underappreciated working class of developed countries – the ones we last left to survive on tea and biscuits – were starting to rebel. **Capitalism** was in crisis, and international **communism** was emerging as an alternative socio-economic system.

In the wake of World War II, the world was left cleaved. Generally the division is thought of as two 'halves' – an established network of capitalist countries, and a younger, struggling communist one. In reality, there were three systems – a **non-aligned movement** also emerged that wanted to foster mutual development while avoiding the pitfalls that came with joining either of the major trade blocs. A variety of blocs also emerged within these three networks, often through the establishment of formal organisations (such as the European Economic Community (EEC)). In time, the world economy became defined in terms of large, multinational trading groups rather than the superior performance of lone nations. This greatly incentivised transnational business, and an explosive rate of growth was seen for multinational corporations. This is a criticism often made of supranational, intergovernmental organisations such as the European Union (EU), which are seen as bedfellows of big business.

The Contemporary World Economy

As the 20th century progressed, cooperation and the de-nationalisation of business continued apace. Capitalist firms were increasingly engaging in the **globalisation** of their operations, abandoning notions that they should have any duty to their home countries, current employees, or neighbours. Of course, matters were only worse for new employee groups, as both physical and cultural distance were used as arguments for even greater worker exploitation. As had been the case since the inception of capitalism, the most important consideration is profit.

As we marched towards the global world economy of today, this is not to say that national power had no role. It did remain in its own way, and in fact had very important effects. Russia used its leadership capacity within the Soviet Union, and throughout the attempted project of global communism, to skew economic relations in their own interests, and in the interests of any other countries they were favouring at a particular moment (e.g. based on geographical and cultural proximity, with Eastern Europe benefiting; or on current loyalty to the USSR). The cooperative potential of socialism, which could have improved quality of life for workers and consumers, was often compromised, and the failure of this project has largely delegitimised those who seek to launch similar initiatives within capitalist countries.

The United States, of course, emerged as a superpower in the post-war period. As the war had not occurred on US territory, and US expenditures were fairly low, it had a natural chance to race to the head of the capitalist pack. The US did what it could to cement these advantages for much time to come. The US dollar became the world trade currency for some time, and though it is not officially anymore, moments like the 2008–2009 Global Financial Crisis reveal that the world is still not ready to let the currency tank. Moreover, the United States is the home of the World Trade Organization (WTO) and the International Monetary Fund (IMF). Though these are meant to be objective, international institutions, they are inevitably influenced by their genesis and placement within the United States. The similarity between US government policy and these organisations is so strong that the policies of the WTO and IMF are often referred to as the 'Washington Consensus'. Sassatelli (2007) notes that this period also saw the rapid expansion of consumer cultures within the US and other developed countries, though enfranchisement was still uneven there. Class differences, it was argued, would encourage people to work harder and achieve the American Dream.

Harvey (2005) argues that the United Kingdom is also a global power in the present. This is because the UK as well as the US made massive gains in the 1980s with the implementation of **neoliberalism** under Thatcherism and Reaganism respectively. This economic doctrine is characterised by rampant privatisation and mass deregulation, impacting workers' and consumers' rights, and largely ending preferential treatment for domestic businesses. If anything, internationalisation was practically incentivised, as the increased margins produced from cheaper, globalised labour were met with less and less restriction via taxation.

In turn, Harvey states that imperialism is alive and well in the present, as these two nations manage to have massive influence over the world economy. This is achieved in three ways. First, via organisations such as the WTO, IMF, and EU, where the US and UK push a particular economic agenda. Second, both nations' superior levels of finance provide them with power that allows them to command the world economy. Finally, as noted by not only Harvey but Parenti (2011), neither country is above the use of military power for furthering their interests.

Parenti provides a particularly harrowing account of how the United States has regularly undermined any government which has sought to resist neoliberalism and the rule of the WTO and IMF. In one of the more shocking examples he considers, he recounts how American agents played a role in short-circuiting Italian communist movements in the 1980s, going so far as to plant bombs in public and blame them on leftist groups, in the interests of keeping labour suppressed within Europe. In the case of the former Yugoslavia, an unwillingness to give up some of the policies of the Soviet era played a key role in the case for military intervention. Iraq, meanwhile, is notable in that it was one of the only countries succeeding to avoid integration into world agricultural trade. Before recent conflicts, it had one of the most organic and sustainable food production systems in the world (not to mention excellent universities and a rich cultural life). Iraq was also interested in increasingly nationalising and socialising the proceeds of the oil industry – which would effectively ring-fence that capital from foreign interests. Parenti reveals the US government documents that cited an economic case for war, long before there was any talk of 'weapons of mass destruction'.

The moment that has most decisively produced the contemporary world economic order is the fall of communism in Europe in the late 1980s. As described by leading continental philosophers Jacques Rancière (1995), Slavoj Žižek (2000), and Alain Badiou (2001), this ushered in a 'post-political' era, wherein communism was so stigmatised that there were no 'political' choices left to be made. Through the powers of the WTO and IMF, we are now at a point where almost all of the world is a part of a single economic system. Evaluations and data from these orgainsations, as well as credit ratings (by Moody's, Fitch, and Standard & Poor), determine countries' eligibility for finance, and terms of debt repayments – with the terms overly punitive for many developing countries.

While the repression of socialist economies was once more piecemeal – as countries and firms sought to stifle the East German economy for example – it can now be done in a well-orchestrated way, mediated by the actions of these non-governmental organisations. Parenti (2011) and Smith (2006) do much to document how structural adjustments and imposed economic policies legitimated via these organisations' evaluations have been used to strangle every major attempt at a socialist government. While it may seem like all this could change if a single strong country sought a major socialist overhaul of their economy – for example, if Corbyn became PM of the UK – we should anticipate a backlash even there. As other countries would still be invested in traditional capitalist economics, and would still have these NGOs at their disposal, we should expect continued pressure – for example, questions about some of Corbyn's envisioned policies.

Where these organisations fail, powerful countries never fail to find a way to achieve what they need. In the case of China, for example, an interest group representing a variety of American businesses (including Apple, Dell, and Nike) was able to quell labour reform attempts that would have significantly improved workers' quality of life, but would have increased the costs of business. The businesses were threatening to leave the country if changes were to be made. This story was obviously not popular within the United States, and is basically unknown, which allows American businesses to persist with a narrative that 'Chinese culture is different' and that 'China does not want reforms' (Ruppel Shell, 2009).

Over time, we have seen some potential cracks within this model of the world economy, outlined by Amin (2004 [1997]). As in the cases of the Irish and Greek financial crises, we saw Germany taking on a leading role within European economic organisation, which it defended based on its own superior economic performance.

The BRIC nations – Brazil, Russia, India, and China – are also on the rise. This is a development that many in developed countries face with apprehension. This anxiety can be both supported and disputed. On the one hand, there is a distinct possibility that one of these countries will engage in the sort of economic machinations that have brought current world powers their position. On the other hand, the

Figure 1.2a   Exhibit showing how various foods are envisioned as commodities for ease of trading. Museum of American Finance, New York. Author's Own.

Figure 1.2b   Exhibit showing how various foods are envisioned as commodities for ease of trading. Museum of American Finance, New York. Author's Own.

rise of the BRIC nations can be viewed as a consciously encouraged policy of these very leaders of the world economy. Put simply, developing these economies in terms of both consumption and production is valuable, as it produces revenue via expenditure and increased efficiency. Supporting workers in these countries also keeps wages in check domestically, while saving money due to the unequal foundation of wage rates. If anything, the BRIC nations may want to watch out, as these firms and nations in the developed world would presumably have a vested interest in contracting consumer and worker standards once again, in the future.

To sum up this section, the world economy can well be understood as a world system with more powerful countries at the **centre**, and others at the **periphery**. Even within central countries and regions, we see **internal colonisation**, as weaker nations (like much of Eastern Europe within the EU) and weaker areas (such as the North of England) are subject to harsh economic treatment that inhibits their competitiveness as well. The system is maintained by strategies of **cultural imperialism** (Said, 1994), which present the economic system of capitalism positively, and encourage the world's population to work extensively for the consumer luxuries enjoyed at the centre. We will explore this more in Chapter 6, on the role of culture.

Meanwhile, there is no such thing as a 'domestic market' anymore. The range of commodities that are traded (or supposedly traded – material objects often do not change hands) globally has increased radically. Figures 1.2a and 1.2b show how even perishable goods are constructed as potential commodities for (real and imagined) trading, as seen on a visit to the Museum of American Finance on Wall Street. This interconnectedness is again reinforced through international organisations, which ensure the maintenance of this economic order. For this reason, even a completely nationally produced product, using domestic labour, is not free from international pressures. The nature of the world's markets for labour, materials, and similar goods touches almost every aspect of economic production in the world.

Again, the uneven distribution of wealth persists to this day. Economists describe the high rates of savings and speculation of the wealthy as *anti-social* in that it provides no actual value to society as a whole; indeed, it actually decreases per capita wealth and happiness (Platteau and Abraham, 2002). Spreading wealth more evenly, especially among those who would gladly consume more, increases expenditure, thus improving gross national product and creating jobs. The system we have now, meanwhile, benefits a very small number of incredibly wealthy individuals.

The Final Word: International Marketing From a Historical Perspective

Taken together, a key strategy of modern international marketing practice is the production of **monopolies**. Firms and nations seek exclusive control over supply of any and all goods it can. This work is conducted both domestically and abroad, but with important nuances in each case. Internationally, the goal is often to be 'the first' or to be so competitive that one can destroy or take over a local market. The introduction of new consumer goods is often used to lure individuals away from farming and traditional production, into the farms and factories of multinationals, despite the fact that the rewards are rarely excellent. Domestically, we see the resale of cheap products sold at high value.

For poorer individuals in developed countries, great outputs of labour may be required for basic survival. For wealthier consumers, cheap goods are sold as luxuries and consumerism is imposed as a social value that encourages maximum participation in the workforce.

While one could say this is the technique of a bygone era, and that things are much better now, this is not often the case. As noted by Amin, the modern global economy can be defined in terms of five monopolies:

- **Technological monopoly**: advanced countries (and firms in them) have the first access to 'necessary' new technologies, leading to significant advantages.
- **Financial control of worldwide markets**: the US-dominated World Bank and IMF provide great control of the industrial power of various nations.
- **Monopolistic access to worldwide natural resources**: very few regulations on the free trade of natural resources.
- **Media and communications monopolies**: television and other media are dominated by countries at the 'global centre', communicating their values outward.
- **Monopolies on violence**: the 'global centre' has a monopoly on military strength, hence no one can fight the system.

In time, the size of these monopolies, and their geographic concentration (in fewer and fewer hands), is only increasing. Branding and other superficial forms of differentiation serve to create *de facto* monopolies among goods that would otherwise be fairly unremarkable commodities. An example could be something as simple as a black T-shirt, which is somehow magically transformed upon the acquisition of a designer label.

It is my hope that this chapter has served its function, in revealing and denaturalising the world organisation of economy. As for what to do with this knowledge, these are matters to be developed throughout the rest of the book.

2

Ethical Stakes

This chapter introduces a new, ethics-based approach for studying international marketing.

To do that, however, one must start by explaining what ethics are. I begin with this duty, and then turn soon thereafter to the task of explaining the relevance of a wide range of schools of ethical thought to our subject. I find that contemporary ethical philosophy, and particularly the work of Alain Badiou (2001), provide radical new insights into the subject of international marketing, so a large section at the end of this chapter explains what Badiou has to offer us.

As noted at the outset, the principle of international marketing at play in this chapter is as follows:

> Principle 2: The ethical stakes of international marketing are often hidden, complicated, and difficult to impact – but comprehending ethics is nevertheless crucial for understanding international marketing practice.

Ultimately, the decisions about ethical and philosophical commitments are yours to make. The point is that your practices will be enhanced with clarity about what your commitments are, and what the implications of them are.

What Are Ethics?

At its most basic level, the field of ethics is a subdiscipline of philosophy.

That's helpful information, but only if you know exactly what philosophy really is, so I'll answer that question too. **Philosophy** is the most abstract form of knowledge production, focused on the big questions of existence (Craig, 2002). Two key components of philosophy, which undergird all other philosophical inquiry, are ontology and epistemology. *Ontology* is focused on defining and understanding what exists, while **epistemology** is concerned with what we can know about that which exists.

Delving deep into these areas would require its own degree programme, so we will not go too deep into these here. For example, some ontologists question whether humans really exist in the physical world, or whether we really move throughout a world of representations. Building on that, they tend to espouse very critical and limited epistemologies, questioning whether an individual can ever really know what others are thinking.

For the time being, I will say that I take a more balanced approach, a sort of **critical realism** proposed by Italian philosopher Maurizio Ferraris (2015, 2014). He accepts the postmodern epistemological principle that our knowledge of reality is imperfect, but says that the ontological existence of a real world means that we must strive to produce knowledge which corresponds to the real world as much as possible. Doing anything else, he argues, would make it impossible for humans to even agree on what a dog or a pair of trousers are – much less something more complicated, like an ethical position. He finds this absurd, given that we do manage to agree on what organisms are classified as dogs, and which are instead birds, and I'm with him on this!

Ethics, meanwhile, refers to questions of value and judgement. In other words, it addresses questions of *what we are to do* with our lives, given *what we know* (epistemology) about *that which exists* (ontology). The need for ethics emerges from the fact that in life there are very often multiple potential actions that can emerge in any situation, and these courses of action vary in terms of their outcomes for a variety of affected parties. In short, we have to make ethical decisions all the time. As noted above, making productive ethical arguments tends to require at least a somewhat realist perspective in the world – a belief that a phenomenon such as labour relations exists, can be defined, and that claims about the phenomenon can be made as we gather increasingly real evidence.

The capacity for ethical reasoning is considered to be a distinctive hallmark of human experience, compared to that of animals (Robinson and Garratt, 2008) – in other words, what makes us different is that we have the ability to think through decisions such as whether we eat meat, whether we kill another living being, or how we alter the natural environment around us. Other animals like dogs are omnivorous, but they do not have a very sophisticated understanding of why they sometimes leap to the table for leftover sausage, and at other times eat our discarded veg. Carnivores, like cats, have no choice but to live off the death of other animals. Beavers, meanwhile are the second most destructive animals compared to humans, but they haven't chosen to be. In this last example, we reach what may be truly distinctive about humans – the fact that we can choose to do harm, even beyond what we need to survive. Perhaps humans have 'more ethical capacity' in that we can do more harm than any other species.

Within ethical philosophy, there are two continua upon which questions vary. The first is that from the **abstract** to the **applied**. The most abstract ethical questions consider issues such as 'what is the good life?' Ancient philosophers were quite taken by these issues and, as such, that's where I will discuss them below. Applied ethics consider questions within very specific domains of life, such as medical ethics, legal ethics, and yes, business ethics. Here, I will not actually use much of the past literature on business ethics, and for good reason. First, good applied ethics should have some connection to more abstract questions. Much of the past literature on business ethics, meanwhile, has unclear or tacit assumptions about the 'big questions' which colour their analyses. Here, I argue instead for a sort of 'mid-range' ethics, which has some view of the 'big questions in life'; considers broader historical contexts (which are discussed elsewhere in the book); and then balances that with the exigencies of more specific human dilemmas.

Why Ethics for International Marketing?

We saw in the previous chapter that marketing practice is as old as commerce and trade. Marketing scholarship, however, is a much more recent phenomenon. It is best dated to the beginning of the 20th century (Jones and Shaw, 2006; Bartels, 1976), and even then, it tended to be little more than unsubstantiated meditations by business practitioners. Flipping through the early years of the *Journal of Marketing*, you will see more articles on transporting milk in the American Midwest than you will articles with any relevance to the world of commerce today. The situation was so bad that the Carnegie and Ford foundations demanded that marketing scholarship step up its game, and that happened in the middle of the 20th century.

Key here was the work of Philip Kotler, which you will undoubtedly have encountered already if you have engaged in marketing study already. I won't re-hash that material here. Instead, I want to bring up some of the points he made for researchers, which are sometimes unknown elsewhere, and are often downplayed even in his key texts like the many editions of *The Principles of Marketing* (from the original (1980) to the 17th (Kotter and Armstrong, 2017)). Put simply, Kotler (along with colleague Sidney Levy) made the daring argument that marketing can – and even should – be applied to a wide range of phenomena, far beyond what commercial marketers would typically consider. They encapsulate the matter thus:

> Marketing ... involves product development, pricing, distribution, and communication; and in the more progressive firms, continuous attention to the changing needs of customers and the development of new products, with product modifications and services to meet these needs ... It is the authors' contention that marketing is a pervasive societal activity that goes considerably beyond the selling of toothpaste, soap, and steel. Political contests remind us that candidates are marketed as well as soap; student recruitment by colleges reminds us that higher education is marketed; and fund raising reminds us that 'causes' are marketed. (Kotler and Levy, 1969: 10)

In doing so, we have three important foundations for marketing (of any sort), and for why thinking of marketing as an ethical practice makes sense. The first is that marketing involves weighing the needs of various social actors (at a minimum, firms and consumers). Second, a wide variety of offerings are marketed, as a result of this groundbreaking proposition. The marketing of a political candidate or a university should be guided by different principles than that of marketing soap. All said, the third, and final consideration is whether this logic is actually true. Can comparatively under-resourced social causes effectively use marketing against their 'competitors' (often firms, governments, etc.)?

As seen in the previous chapter on history, international marketing is a particularly complicated terrain. The economic relationships which produce the international marketplace are a result of long and often controversial historical processes. Contestations not only between consumers and producers, but also between global, regional, and local producers, can be heated. Ultimately, I find using proper ethical deliberation can help us understand the true nature of the complicated matters at hand. In turn, this can improve the sorts of decisions that marketers make – regardless of the type of marketing challenge sought.

In the sections that follow, I present valuable points from all eras of European philosophy, from the ancient to the present. Here, I must note that this is a practical, rather than an objectively justifiable decision, guided by the fact that this is the intellectual tradition from which most UK academics (like myself) hail. Producing parallel versions of this text grounded in other philosophical traditions (e.g. Chinese philosophy, African philosophy, Middle Eastern philosophy, and Latin American philosophy) would be equally valuable and worthwhile.

Introducing Ancient Ethics

You would be surprised to hear this, but the ancient Greek philosophers had something to say about the ethics of marketing! They were not particularly attendant to issues of internationalisation, but still, their thoughts are important to further work on the ethics of marketing – of any sort. That said, it is not only these couple of nuggets of insight that we will be using. Indeed, a variety of very foundational, abstract principles from ethical philosophy have implications for marketing research and practice. I begin by introducing those here, before moving on to the few comments the ancient philosophers made on marketing.

To begin, the three greatest figures of Ancient Greek philosophy are generally agreed to be Socrates, Plato, and Aristotle. These three were an 'academic family' of sorts, with Socrates as the 'grandfather' down to Aristotle as the 'grandson'. While Socrates did not leave physical writings, we have learned about his interventions through his students. Socrates is believed to have pioneered the notion of 'dialogues' as a form of knowledge production. Here, the idea is that the best knowledge will be produced by a group, and that even the leader of the dialogue should be open to the notion that they do not know everything about a topic. This is where my emphasis on 'forgetting everything' you *think* you know comes from – we all can learn more from rethinking areas, even if we think we are expert within them.

A second important intervention of Socrates' is the notion that knowledge needs to be produced starting from the student's perspective and past knowledge, with teachers tasked to gradually bring them closer to intended answers (when there are intended/known answers). At times, the questioner would even feign ignorance, asking the student to jump ahead and give an advanced account, so that the teacher could understand a student's (potentially misleading) preconceptions. In allowing students to co-create the knowledge, and to see it self-referentially, deeper and more valuable learning is thought to be produced. That is why I ask you to consider questions from your own perspective throughout this text.

Socrates' third idea was that even very abstract, complicated matters can be understood by moving upwards in abstraction, very gradually. By slowly increasing the level of abstraction involved in your study, you can arrive at deeper and more contextualised understandings of the matters at hand. This is a counterpoint to the notion that one should jump quickly from a case to a potential theory. The risk there is that the theory is not truly best and well connected to the context of interest. His final, related notion is that 'the unexamined life is not worth living' – in other words, that developing knowledge of the world around us is inherently useful, as it advances our own lives as well as that of those around us. While this may sound pretty prosaic, the ruling class saw all this questioning as so dangerous that Socrates was executed.

Socrates' intellectual 'son' Plato built upon this, arguing that while individuals frequently think they know the world around them, true understanding is only possible by abstraction. He noted that many are convinced by powerful actors *not* to engage in this sort of thought, because they can easily be controlled if they are ignorant. Take a moment to consider some of the many examples of this today.Plato's alternative idea of society was that it should be ruled by 'philosopher kings' – those who love knowledge, and who will promote a realistic (and therefore maximally valuable) portrait of the world around us. There was some concern about the actual value of democracy, given that average people are somewhat unlearned. When they took over governments, it was seen to be just as problematic as when military, clergy, commerce, or aristocracy ruled. This remains one of the most controversial conclusions from Plato's work.

Aristotle attempted to systematise the knowledge production principles of Socrates and Plato. He stressed the value of moving not only from the world to theory, but then back again – in other words, stressing deduction as well as induction. He believed that there was value to building upon what had previously been known, in order to understand the world around us, as well as trying to start from scratch in every situation. In other words, he contends that the best knowledge can be produced by moving both upwards and downwards throughout the hierarchy of knowledge production. Taken together, the Ancient Greek tradition of philosophy is seen as foundational to both scientific and social scientific forms of knowledge production, as well as philosophy.

Aristotle is particularly notable in that he was the most interested of the three in ethics. He is the originator of the notion that humans are unique within the animal kingdom because of their ethical capacity—and not simply the presence of opposable thumbs! This means that we have choices, and we do prioritise our lives around cooperative social and cultural projects in a way that animals do not. We have the ability to significantly impact the environment around us, by deploying this reasoning. Of course, as we discussed earlier, this might just mean that we can also be more evil, but that is another matter...

His ethics are grounded in the notion of **virtue**. He argues that virtuous people are those that seek to enhance their own happiness, and those around them. People who are not virtuous have warped and problematic worldviews, producing chaos rather than order. In short, he viewed ethics as a **choice** of an individual, and as such, representative of an individual's characteristics. Finally, he believed that ethics are worthless unless they are put into **practice** – in other words, he exhorted the importance of activating individuals, in cases where they know that certain outcomes would be better or worse for those around them.

Recognition of the Value of Ancient Ethics in… Marketing Scholarship!

Reference to the importance of ancient ethics can be found as early as the first year of the *Journal of Marketing* (Cassels, 1936). There, and in other treatments, it is noted that these philosophers raise major questions about business matters that we now consider mundane. In key publications, Plato is often taken as a starting point. Again, he believed society is best run by those who love knowledge and aspire to guard the peace of society. He raises questions about the role of commerce within society, ultimately arguing that those who seek to exaggerate the values of products are a threat to democracy, and perhaps should not be citizens of Athens… with the potential that they should be cast out and left to live in exile! He went so far as to say:

> 'Puffery' or 'praising the goods' was ranked as a crime of lesser magnitude but in the same class as adulteration of products, as is shown by the following: 'He who sells anything in the agora (market) shall not ask two prices for that which he sells, but he shall ask one price … and there shall be no praising of any goods, or oath taken about them. If a person disobey this command, any citizen who is present, not being less than thirty years of age, may with impunity chastize and beat the swearer'. (*Dialogues of Plato*, 1937: 917–920, quoted in Kelley, 1956: 63)

So in other words, he advocated for corporal punishment for those who exaggerate the claims of their products. This might seem extreme, but you may sympathise if you think of a few advertisements that you feel went too far and targeted vulnerable customers, such as the elderly, for example. He also was very against the idea of **price discrimination** – charging two different prices for the same product – which is considered to be a key strategy in contemporary marketing. Within the UK, we entirely accept the notion that hotels, trains, and planes, for example, can charge a wide range of prices for what is essentially the same service. There are particularly interesting international implications as well, given that consumers in the first world are often charged more for goods than their counterparts in the developing world. If this were to be re-invested and used to help their poorer contemporaries, that would be one thing, but often times these 'price premiums' exist solely to increase private profits. Plato is also credited with the following:

> Plato rather scornfully assigns the tasks of storekeeper and sales-man to the infirm: 'In well ordered states they are commonly those who are the weakest in bodily strength, and therefore of little use for any other purpose...'. In 'The Laws,' Plato characterizes a city of merchants and shopkeepers as 'unfriendly and unfaithful both to her own citizens and to other nations.' (Quoted in Steiner, 1976: 2, referring to Plato's 'The Republic' and Plato's 'The Laws', respectively).

Aristotle, meanwhile, argued that:

> 'Of the two sorts of money-making, as I have just said, one is a part of household management, the other is retail trade: the former is necessary and honorable, the latter a kind of exchange which is justly censured; for it is unnatural, and a mode by which men gain from one another' and also that 'Those who buy to sell again as soon as they can are to be accounted as vulgar; for they can make no profit except by a certain amount of falsehood, and nothing is meaner than falsehood'. (Both from Aristotle's 'Politics', quoted by Kelley, 1956: 63)

Aristotle thought that farming and production were natural, good, basic human endeavours, while acquisition and exchange were viewed as corrupt (Steiner, 1976). This is because he saw consumer and firm interests as opposed, and as such, exchange as inherently competitive and inefficient.

Modern Philosophy: Meditations on Means vs. Ends

Ancient ethics are often called 'virtue ethics' after Aristotle, given the emphasis on human nature and differences in individual character. Within modern philosophy, two movements are particularly relevant to students of international marketing: **consequentialism** (ethics defined by ends) and **deontology** (ethics evaluated in terms of means). **Pragmatism** is also notable, as it serves as a sort of reconciliation between the two. I discuss these movements in turn, here.

A key consequentialist tradition is **utilitarianism** – the notion that we should pursue 'the greatest good for the greatest number', at times by any means possible. This was a radical turn from virtue ethics, given the de-prioritisation of individual character and intention. Jeremy Bentham was a key thinker here. He believed that if individuals pursued their own happiness, this would also lead to collective happiness. In particular, he was interested in seeing the liberation of the poor, women, slaves, and animals come to fruition.

There is, of course, a fairly obvious problem with Bentham's approach to utilitarianism – namely, the fact that an individual's pleasure and what is good with society are sometimes at odds. This is where John Stuart Mill comes into the picture. He argues that some utilities are more valuable than others, and that those which fulfil collective as well as individual utility are best. Moreover, he found that individuals aren't actually good at assessing outcomes, so he argues that we usually live by *rules*, which we believe will lead to particular outcomes. This can be seen as a turn towards deontology, from consequentialism.

Immanuel Kant is considered to be the key thinker of deontology, going so far as to say that the means are more important than the ends. The idea here is that if we judged individuals (and firms!) only by consequences, this would not necessarily incentivise good behaviour going forward, as the consequences obtained could have been from chance. Focusing on encouraging good means, meanwhile, is argued to be a more consistent way to create good behaviour.

John Dewey sought to contribute to the conversation with his work on pragmatic ethics. Here, he argued that ethics evolve as not only individuals but also societies test hypotheses, and refine with experience. Harking back to the work of Aristotle, ethical deliberation is seen to be neither exclusively inductive nor deductive, but rather an iterative process which functions best when using both abstraction and cases. While pragmatism is often remembered as being very applied and disinterested in identifying the 'big principles' by which we live, this was not the original intention; instead, the idea is that we are doing the best we can, and that we can collectively improve our behaviour over time.

In terms of the consequentialism vs. deontology debate, this can be seen as making recourse to both outcomes (ends) as well as principles (duties, means). In time, this perspective has proved most useful, as many individuals, organisations, and governments employ systems which evaluate *both* means and ends. For example, many contemporary business regulation systems employ such an approach, to ensure that companies are neither engaging in bad means, nor achieving below-par outcomes. This maximises the value of each perspective, while ameliorating their shortcomings.

Universalisability vs. Relativism

There is one other notion of Kant's which merits mention, before moving forward. Kant is credited with the notion that 'all humans are ends in themselves', meaning that they should not be used as a means to some other goal. In other words, a modicum of individual autonomy is not to be violated in order to improve the lot of the masses. This may sound abstract, but it has major implications, for example in medical ethics. Previously, some medical and pharmaceutical research had been done without consent or adequate compensation, based on arguments that allowing some to suffer would ultimately be the best thing for humans as a whole. A Kantian perspective would argue that adequate information and compensation must be offered, in order to ensure that the compromise of the individual is recouped.

Via this move, Kant became a leading proponent of **universalisability**, or the idea of **absolutist** (absolutely applicable) ethics. Here, the idea is that the 'goodness' of someone's intention can be assessed based on whether they would apply their ethical rules universally. This is particularly relevant for international marketing, as we see firms often engage in dubious forms of **relativism**, saying that potentially unethical business practices are acceptable in other contexts, given the different cultural standards at play. Kant would disagree, saying that if you would not do something to your family or your neighbours, you probably shouldn't be doing it at all!

Modern Ethics and Marketing

Beyond the abstract philosophical contributions noted above, which have inherent value to international marketing practitioners (and people in general!), modern philosophy also had some more specific pronouncements, related to the conduct of international business.

The most frequently referenced touchpoints can be found in moral philosophy. The term **moral philosophy** is used to describe 19th century ethicists (Robinson and Garratt, 2008), who were writing at the moment where modern industrial capitalism and the global division of labour were just emerging – historical developments which merited new ethical considerations. This generation of philosophers found the guidance of ancient and early modern philosophy to be limiting, given how little it discussed commerce, and how negative it was when it did. It is notable here that modern moral philosophers working from a capitalist bent decided to do just the opposite – to start with an inherent bias towards commerce. Elsewhere, Marx was quite descriptive in *Capital* (1867), though he and Engels are undeniably critical in *The Communist Manifesto* (1848). Here, and throughout our investigations into philosophy, it is important to be conscious of the assumptions of writers; to assess the quality of argument in terms of the ethical deliberation entailed; and to reconcile this with your own perspective.

One key modern moral economist was Adam Smith, who of course attended to questions of how international provisioning systems should be structured in his *Wealth of Nations* (1776). This is considered to be the most notable exhortation of the idea that different countries and cultures have varying abilities and potential contributions – and in doing so, he provided a philosophical justification for the international division of labour. As we saw in Chapter 1, abilities were not as unequally distributed as thinkers like Smith believed, and this perspective has been seen retrospectively to be very self-serving.

A nascent critique of this perspective appears in Marx's (1867) work on **original accumulation of capital,** the notion that modern capitalist economic systems depended on the claiming and enclosure (privatisation) of resources which were once deemed public and collective. In other words, the existence of various families, groups, and societies which had amassed unusually large amounts of wealth is understood instead in terms of their willingness to capture, enclose, and speculate upon that which once would have been considered collective. Put simply, Marx reminds us of the uncomfortable fact that there was no legitimate, or even legal justification for early systems of capital accumulation.

Much less-known is Smith's *Theory of Moral Sentiments* (1759). While this work came first, he kept working on it throughout his life, and thought of it as his greatest work. In it, he countered many of the claims made in *The Wealth of Nations*, arguing that while individuals could act in terms of *self-interest*, they should instead operate based on the unique human capacity of *sympathy* for others.

Malthus (1798), meanwhile, was concerned with how growing and urbanising populations could be provided for, as workers left farms for factories. Over time, Malthusian moral philosophy has been deployed for both very progressive and nefarious ends. For example, the notion that women should have some control over how many children they have is a Malthusian idea, which offers not only autonomy to women, but also control of the size of populations, which benefits all. At the same time, Malthusian arguments have been used to justify some of the darkest aspects of human behaviour such as genocide (see the example in Niazi, 2005).

Given these moral philosophers' emphasis on commerce, this tradition was foundational to the field of economics, so much so that early economists generally thought of themselves as moral philosophers. This is interesting, given that contemporary economists tend to deflect matters of ethical deliberation. More on that later... For now, what we need to talk about is the work of Alfred Marshall (1890). He sought to bring together the work of moral philosophers such as Smith and Mill to argue that the most efficient social organisation is possible when supply and demand determine the functioning of provisioning systems. In other words, this is the principle of 'letting the market decide'. Marshall diverged from Mill, arguing instead that utility can be quite easily quantified, and that individuals *know* how much value they get from any purchase.

It is interesting here to note that Marshall's conceptualisation of **consumer demand** places individual buyers as sort of 'kings' within market systems. In other words, he believed that businesses cannot supply that which people do not want to buy. While this was a worthwhile initial proposition – certainly at the time, when marketing was not very sophisticated – we have seen since that consumers are very often encouraged to buy things they would have never imagined, and for which they have no need. We need only watch one episode of *Mad Men* to see that markets, especially in the post-war era, are created and desires manufactured. In addition, this unrealistic position is needlessly disempowering for businesses, as it downplays the power they actually have, and asks firms to focus on some sort of magic, non-existent will of consumers which needs to be animated. Taken together, the critique of Marshall's notion of demand is perhaps best made by 20th century institutional economist John Kenneth Galbraith, who found that 'No significant manufacturer introduces a new product without cultivating the consumer demand for it' (quoted in Palmer, 2009). The formula milk case from the previous chapter is a perfect example of this phenomenon, as it was introduced despite the fact that there was no pre-existing demand for it.

Coolsen (1960), looking back, proposes that marketing can perhaps be understood as emerging from German liberal capitalist economics, which thought that capitalism would ultimately bring the most prosperity. As we have seen from Chapter 1, there are some serious concerns about whether that has actually happened, and there are many cases where marketing was used under socialism. There is also, once again, Kotler's notion that marketing could be applied to non-capitalist causes, even within capitalist countries. Another notable marketing scholar, Shelby Hunt, engaged in a decades-long interchange with Kotler on the matter, contesting that marketing is indeed best understood as capitalist. In the end, he ultimately accepted that it could be non-profit, but that it is always competitive (Hunt and Morgan, 1995) – defined in terms of deploying superior resources (finance, creativity) in order to present a 'winning' value proposition for consumers.

Moral Philosophy in the 20th Century

Ultimately, the subsumption of ethics into moral philosophy, and then moral philosophy into economics, meant that ethics in the beginning of the 20th century were largely defined by the sort of economic philosophy one adhered to. Were you a capitalist, or a Marxist? Regardless of one's orientation, many 'forgot' that they were engaging in ethical deliberations at all in time, as they focused on the pragmatic consequences that emanated from their original decisions about which camp to join. Ask your average economist or marketer now if they are master ethicists, engaging in complicated deliberations daily, and they will look at you as if you have two heads. This is, however, the point of this book – to identify the hidden foundations of contemporary business practice, and then use this to enhance what we do – whatever that is.

Capitalist moral philosophy (in the guise of neoclassical economics) became particularly focused on the details of how systems, firms, and individuals act to create ideal markets, or engage in abnormal behaviour, which suppresses the functioning of perfect competition. In time, companies rejected the notion of consumer sovereignty (autonomy of demand) and, as we discussed in Chapter 1, have adopted a neoliberal approach wherein the possibility of shaping demand is not only assumed but also seen as inherently good – at least for businesses. In comparison to the neoliberal tradition, the classical and neoclassical traditions seem practically pro-social, in that they believed that well-functioning (though private) market systems would result in the most productive and just distributions of prices and wages. The ideal of perfect information, which urged firms to inform customers thoroughly of a product's benefits and limitations, has been all but brushed aside, as exaggerating a product's benefits is now taken for granted. In doing so, neoliberalism has let go of the responsibility for developing a system which will best benefit society, and has instead proposed an ethic which celebrates the individual's right to private profit.

Marxism, too, evolved within the 20th century. The **critical theory** tradition, dominated by the Frankfurt School of philosophers, sought to improve upon some limitations of Marx's original works. In particular, they found that Marxist philosophy could not adequately explain the role of culture in legitimating capitalism, nor the ways in which capitalism commodifies and sells culture. Adorno and Horkheimer provide one of the best encapsulations of this in their *Dialectic of Enlightenment* (1947), which contended that a **culture industry** has emerged to serve both functions. They are often noted (and criticised) for their at times over-zealous denunciations of popular culture, in favour of arts which require significantly more effort to appreciate (and thus, ironically, more class). Writing slightly earlier, Italian philosopher Antonio Gramsci (1925–1935) used the term **soft power** to describe how people come to be controlled via culture, rather than brute force means such as imprisonment and physical violence, and French philosopher Guy Debord later described a **society of spectacle** which was built upon American-influenced commodities, advertising and mass media. More recently, another Marxist thinker, Jodi Dean, has used the term **communicative capitalism** to describe the ways in which the neoliberal order is reinforced through the very means of new media and technologies that claim to create change.

Keynesianism, meanwhile, emerged as a middle-ground choice, existing in the space between strictly capitalist or socialist options (Keynes, 1936). Keynesian economists advocate for a moderate level of government intervention via taxation and policy, as this was argued to be the most reasonable method for consistently assuring the provision of social goods like healthcare, education, and welfare. It also identified many of the flaws in classical economic theories, which tended to not work properly in practice (Temin and Vines, 2014).

In many ways, Keynesian philosophies were foundational to the government structures of most countries today, and can be seen as valuable for these reasons. They have even experienced a resurgence since at the same time, these moderate perspectives can be seen as quite unprincipled, as they ultimately do not take a strong position on the value of business. Put differently, they allow for levels of wealth privatisation that many on the left would view as anti-social and ultimately negative for the population as a whole (Ali, 2018). Free market purists and libertarians on the right, meanwhile, continue to argue that any interventions by government would make economic systems less efficient.

This containment of ethics within economic perspectives was generally deemed acceptable for much of the 20th century. Within the United States, there was a conscious effort to depose Marxist and critical philosophers from the academy during the McCarthy era, and this had a lasting impact on American scholarship right through to today where 'Cultural Marxism' is used as a popular derogatory slur. **Postmodern** philosophers there, and in Europe, turned their attention to the limitations of Marxism and critical theory. They saw within it a sort of intellectual straight-jacket, in its theorising of an all-powerful state. Foucault, in his early works, focused on the fact that a wide range of individuals become 'carriers' of the oppressive messages of governments and business, doing the dirty work for them. If the world is terrible, we were all to be terrible. Similarly, Bourdieu using his concept of **habitus** argued that structures such as the state were dialectically entwined with human agency through daily practices in a given field whereby one develops 'a feel for the game'. Others, like Derrida, Baudrillard, and Lyotard became fixated on the question of whether or not we can ever know what another is thinking. In turn, they tended to treat the possibility of ethical deliberation or collective social action with suspicion. Through these and other arguments, contemporary philosopher Maurizio Ferraris (2015, 2012) argues that within this vacuum of power, the comparatively organised capitalist camp came to dominate the landscape of 20th century ethical deliberation, legitimating neoliberal perspectives along the way.

The containment of ethics within economics, and within a single neoliberal consensus, was not, however, infinitely sustainable…

Ethics Escapes Economics

In Foucault's last works, which were often presented in lectures as he was dying, he became troubled by his earlier pronouncements that we are all complicit in structures of power. Here, he reconsidered the nature of **responsibility**, finding that many individuals have little knowledge of how they have been made complicit, and thereby placing a much greater amount of ethical responsibility upon the most powerful actors within society.

Foucault unfortunately died before he was able to complete his intellectual project, so we will never know exactly where this work was to end. What we do know, however, is that many of his contemporaries have taken up the mantle. A powerful subsection of the generation of European philosophers who have been active from the 1960s to the present have focused specifically on the question of how social change may be *possible*, even if not *probable* (Agamben, 2009, 1999).

Moreover, they have radically redefined our notion of what an individual is. Here, they have moved away from the notion that each individual has a consciousness as important as the consciousness of all others, to the sense that some have much more power (and hence responsibility) than others. Their work can be seen as tacitly drawing on Sartre's particular blend of **existentialism,** which focused not only on an individual's existence and choices, but also on how those choices are constrained by our social surroundings (something Sartre refers to as **facticity** or 'facts' about who we are; Sartre, 2003 [1943]). Also influential here is the work of later psychoanalysts like Lacan, who contend that our psyche is largely a product of society, family, and culture, rather than inborn tendencies or chosen sentiments (Hallward, 2001).

Building on this, these contemporary philosophers argue that most individuals have **subjectivity** rather than identity – in other words, their sense of who they are is a product of the many socio-political (as well as idiosyncratic) forces a person has been subjected to within their lifetime. Rather than focusing on the Aristotelian notion of an individual and their virtue, we see individuals as not very important at all. What are more important are the systems by which ethical education occurs. As such, ethics emerge as a dimension of society rather than individuals, with 'bad ethics' coming from bad societies.

Contemporary Close-Up: Badiouian Ethics

Particularly relevant and prolific to these discussions is Alain Badiou. Across his major works, and best summarised in his *Ethics* (2001), Badiou argues that there are essentially three ethical positions within society. We have those who are **evil,** who know the truth about how society functions and use it to fulfil only their self-interest; those who are **good,** and act pro-socially despite knowing enough to do otherwise; and those who are **neither.** While this may be logical enough, perhaps the greater contribution comes from what Badiou does with this typology. He urges us not to get distracted by hating those who are neither, as he views them as largely 'irresponsible' for their actions. Instead, those who know better should focus on contesting the self-interested dominance of bad actors within society.

The question that you would expect would plague Badiou is what to do about the fact that the powerful are... well... powerful! Here, Badiou has a unique explanation, which he has fleshed out much more significantly than any of his contemporaries. He argues that there are rare moments – which he calls **events** – wherein powerful actors *momentarily* fail in their ability to *subjectivate* individuals. Key examples are during the Egyptian revolution, or in the wake of the Global Financial Crisis of 2008–2009. In these moments, people have a rare glimpse at 'the man behind the curtain', and could be convinced to act differently than they previously had. Except in the case of major revolutions, there is rarely a complete reversal of the ethical order of society, but even smaller events are of use, as the will to present an alternative ethics can be produced successively, over time.

This perspective has some big implications for those who want to engage in business ethics – and those that contest the work of businesses. First, business ethics are seen to be quite derivative: they are pretty much just doing the work of the system around us. Second, it raises big questions about the complicity of consumers. From a Badiouian perspective, we see choices about whether to be 'green' or how much meat to eat not as individual decisions, but as consequences of major socio-political processes. This means that the ultimate responsibility for macro-level social problems (e.g. hunger, sustainability) is in the hands of business and government, rather than individuals. In other words, there is no sense that 'every conscience is equal', as not every person can have the same effect within the world around them. Finally, business is seen as a part of that which makes life more miserable, on the whole; I will discuss this matter at more length in the final closing to this chapter.

The Final Word: Why It's Worth Thinking of International Marketing in Terms of Ethics

There are two main reasons why ethics *should* be a foundation of international marketing scholarship and practice – even if that has not been historically the case.

The first reason is that there is an inherent, ethical decision to marketing practice. We need to ask questions about who we are marketing for. Whose interests are we trying to serve? Does it truly improve the lives of our customers? What do we believe about society, and the role of commerce within it? What sorts of practices do we think are justifiable, and not justifiable, as a result? Where there are competing interests, how do we balance them? How much respect and autonomy do we afford to competing parties? Are we willing to do things to customers that we would not want done to ourselves? Are we willing to accept practices in production and sourcing that we would not want to expose ourselves and our families to?

Any time there is a decision such as this, which has to balance a variety of individuals' perspectives, an ethical decision is made. This is the case even if a marketer is not aware that there is an ethical dimension. Indeed, this was a matter that Sparks and Hunt (1998) helpfully illuminated, as they found that marketers are frequently completely unaware of this, and with that in mind *building awareness* is the first step towards facilitating more effective marketing practice. And again, ethical deliberation is valuable not only for touchy-feely, socially responsible industries, but also for any marketer, as engaging in unethical practices may very well backfire. In cases where an unethical practice is so widespread that people hardly bat an eye, Chapter 1 should serve as a reminder that our expectations and standards can change faster than we would think.

As you can imagine from reading Chapter 1, these matters are only more pronounced in the case of international marketing. There are complicated questions concerning why particular trade relations exist at all. Common international marketing practices such as mergers and acquisitions (often leading to the dissolution of local labour forces) can be quite unpopular on the ground. Moreover, power differentials can be incredibly large across international boundaries, with global industry leaders able to easily trounce local firms, even if it only makes a marginal improvement in the global firm's performance. Here, there are questions of what sorts of human costs are acceptable, in exchange for what financial rewards. Finally, as I will discuss in Chapter 5, there are major issues in dealing with customers across international and intercultural lines, as one's target markets may have marked differences in education, access to information and ability to understand marketing communications. Why and how one deals with stakeholder groups such as this are major issues to consider.

The second reason for an ethical approach is that there are in fact identifiable ethical principles with which decisions can be made. While international marketing contexts may be complex, there are analyses that can be performed. In producing some guidance on the matter, it is helpful to refer to the work of Jones et al. (2005), who performed a similar exercise for business ethics more generally. They explain the potential uses of consequentialism and deontology, similarly arguing for a combined approach. That is one principle from which to start. Then, they discuss matters of how to balance what one believes about individuals, their autonomy, and their needs, with the world as it is.

Here, I like to take their work farther, and in a different direction, informed by the Badiouian philosophy which has only emerged more recently. Put simply, Badiou argues that those who know how the world functions, and use it in their own interests, are engaging in poor ethics. This is not only because it puts self-interest ahead of social interests – a concern of both the consequentialist and deontological camps. The bigger issue is that engaging in bad practice is a lot of work for everyone! This is what can be described as a *liberatory* ethic, and it is one which began in Marxism, moves through critical theory, and returns to this day.

Here's one way to think of it: it may be helpful to think that for every marketer who is selling fast food or candy or cigarettes to children, there are dozens of other marketers also selling equally tempting, equally unneeded or anti-social products to them. Indeed, if we think of the contemporary economy as a system, we see that it is not really in anyone's interests – or at the very least, only a handful of people benefit from it the most. An interesting illustration of this can be seen in economic work on conspicuous consumption, which shows that it is an unending game – one in which most of us participate, but only those with the absolute highest consumption can feel confident within. Even then, there is always something new to buy...

Of course, that is just one perspective, and your evaluation of it may vary. For example, you may find that you get disproportionate joy out of competition compared to others – that 'winning' in marketing is really winning for you, for some reason. Or you simply may not care – you may decide that if this is the game, you would like to play it. At the end of the day, this and all other decisions are yours to make. The important point is that there is a decision to be made, and that life, and marketing, are done best when we act knowing this.

3

Political Nature

Business research has traditionally made little use of the discipline of politics. This is a real tragedy, as business itself is a form of politics. This chapter introduces readers to the discipline of politics, conceptualising its value for the study of international marketing.

As with previous chapters, I will begin by introducing what this discipline does. This work is all the more important where politics are concerned, as we have so many common-sense ideas about what politics are. It's such important work that it would be helpful for you to take a moment to reflect upon your pre-existing knowledge and ideas about politics. Doing so will facilitate your understanding of the discussion of definitional issues which follows.

What do politics mean to you?

....
....
....
....
....
....
....
....
....
....
....
....
....
....

What you just did, in research methods terms, is called **bracketing**. It refers to processes where we take a moment to identify and put aside what we personally think about a subject, before jumping into a discussion of what some phenomenon means to a wider audience (e.g. to those invested in it), or what it *should* mean (i.e. what is the most *analytically useful* definition). As you will see, some of our everyday ideas about politics do have relevance and traction for understanding international marketing, while others may be of less utility.

> Once we can agree on what politics are in the abstract – even if we can't agree on political positions! – we can start the work of identifying what politics as a discipline can do for international marketing. Politics is a large and diverse field of social inquiry, so I focus my attention on those traditions and methods which are most useful to this task. As stated at the outset, the takeaway of this chapter is as follows:

> Principle 3: As international marketing is an exercise of power, it is inherently political.

Right now, you may be wondering why this is the case. How can it be that international marketing is *always* political? Isn't politics just something for organisations like Greenpeace? Do they even do marketing? Is it even international? If I'm interested in for-profit work, why should I care about politics?

Rest assured that all will be revealed, in due course. Why international marketing is political is something that makes sense when we understand what politics really are. Interestingly, we will see that the principle above has as much relevance for traditional commerce as it does for activism or social marketing. So, without further ado…

What Are Politics?

The 'core' notion of what politics are, in a social science sense, has been articulated by so many people and in so many ways… many of them quite boring. I find that one of the most evocative explanations actually comes from a communications researcher, Harold Lasswell. He famously characterised politics as 'who gets what, when, and how' (1936). Key to understanding this statement, or any other on the subject, is the notion of power. **Power** refers to the ability of an individual or an institution to effectuate change in other individuals or institutions. Aside from a handful of remaining hunter-gatherer tribes which have a non-hierarchical form of social arrangement, all contemporary societies are characterised by differences in status and power among its people. Some people have more sway over the actions of others, and as such those in power drive the 'who, what, when, and how' of everything in society, culture, and economy.

While Lasswell's words are evocative, they would get unwieldy in practice. Building on similar premises, Dahl provides one of the clearest (though perhaps a bit less interesting) definitions of politics. He says that political systems are 'any persistent pattern of human relationships that involves, to a significant extent, power, rule, or authority' (1970). Here, Dahl and other politics researchers are interested in how we have arrived at a state where power imbalances exist, and how those in power maintain or reform the very systems that brought them into that position. As one would imagine, this often involves considering history, but again for the moment we will try to keep the disciplines as distinct as possible.

As for the point of why it is specifically relevant to international marketing, that can be answered easily enough, though we do need to add a few more concepts. To start, we have to define what an economy is. The term **economy** refers to any system of resource distribution. More or less every human society has some sort of economy, and economies exist at smaller scales too – for example, household economies within families (Carruthers and Babb, 2013; Swedberg, 2003). The terms **market** and **market economy** refer to systems where goods and services are privatised. Individuals need to sell their labour in order to get items they need or want. Usually, though not always, labour and goods are exchanged for **currency (money)**. Market systems are structured and influenced by differences in power and access to resources. In other words, some actors have much more of a say about 'who gets what, when, and how'. As such, markets are inherently political systems.

With the rudimentary definitional matters out of the way, we can now move on to the rest of the chapter, which will tell us how politics are studied, including some preliminary uses within marketing. Most of these past uses were not tailored to international marketing, however, so the conclusion establishes the foundations for a politics-informed approach to international marketing. From this, as well as the parallel sections from Chapters 1 and 2, you will be ready for Part 2 (which reconsiders international marketing practice based on these foundations), and Part 3 (which considers the contexts and futures of new media and sustainability).

Before we start, however, it may be helpful to consider the following question by yourself. Like all questions in this book, it is fine to think through this based on a basic, everyday background knowledge of international marketing as a field of business practice.

> Using this new definition of politics, what do you think may be some political aspects of international marketing?

....

....

....

....

....

....

....

....

....

....

....

....

....

Methods of Studying Politics

The political analysis methods presented here aren't just for scholars. They can be used in business, political organising, or even just as a regular individual. The first approach can be described as **political philosophy**. Given that we already know what philosophy is – as defined in Chapter 2, it is the method of inquiry interested in the broadest possible discussions within major domains of human experience – the next step is presumably to identify what that means within the study of politics. Political philosophy considers 'big questions' related to the nature of power, government, social order, organisation, and responsibility.

Political theory exists one step down, and seeks to develop knowledge between the most abstract and most concrete levels – what some in marketing research have defined as 'meso-level' knowledge (Askegaard and Linnet, 2011). This is not to say that political theory analysis requires only one level of knowledge; in reality, it requires the ability to nimbly jump from very abstract matters to everyday life, and then to find the compromise in between. **Political analysis,** often referred to as **political science** within the United States, can be one step further towards the 'concrete'. In other words, it often maintains a primary interest in applying theory within a very specific context – for example, understanding which of two business strategies will be superior given particular considerations. **Political economy,** meanwhile, seeks to understand political dimensions of economic organisation. It can address debates about the nature of comparatively socialist and capitalist policies, for example. It also provides insight into the nature and composition of specific types of economy, such as the political economy of media ownership.

Critical discourse analysis, finally, seeks to understand the nature of power in shaping language. Scholars using this method draw upon their own knowledge of politics to analyse any piece of text. They may also interrogate the **positionality** (place in a social order) of an author or speaker, so as to understand the ways in which they hold power. For example, a critical discourse analysis of a politician's speech would be interested in their place within the political sphere (is it a Prime Minister or a back-bencher?), and then might consider what sorts of political positions/concepts are being deployed by the speaker (is an appeal fiscally conservative?).

Again, the sections that follow are focused on introducing various intellectual traditions which have shed light on the politics of marketing practice. Unless stated otherwise, these approaches tend to be at the level of political theory, as the goal is the development of meso-level knowledge which can be applied in a variety of situations. Using these theories in a specific business context (e.g. your own work) would then be more akin to political analysis, as political analysis is very applied in nature. At the end of the day, not only do all of the theories here have clear implications for international marketing, but considering the international context also provides us with the opportunity to further develop nascent understandings of marketing as inherently political.

French and Raven's Bases of Power

A helpful framework – and one of the only explicitly political approaches which has been used in marketing research – is that of French and Raven's (summarised in Raven, 1965) **bases of power.** These social scientists proposed that power is not simply one thing, but comes in a variety of types, each of which is defined by – you guessed it! – its basis.

The first is **coercive power**, wherein the threat of force is used to gain control over another party. While this is obviously the reason why physical violence is an effective political tactic, it should be noted that force could be exerted via economic or social channels, as well as through physical harm or sabotage. Then we see **reward power** – when one party can give another something they really want. This can be seen as a 'carrot' rather than 'stick' strategy, in that it emphasises positive rather than negative outcomes. From parenting to business, it is consistently found that humans are more receptive to reward power than coercive power. Also well received is **legitimate power**, which is based on widely agreed upon authority. An example here is government, which the majority believe is necessary and acting (at least at a minimum level) in the interests of society. **Information-based power** exists when one party has information that another wants.

Reference power exists when one party has power over another, because the latter wants to be like the former. We see this in the relationships between younger children and their older siblings, for example. A business application of this could be where a smaller firm or consultant accepts doing poorly compensated – or even free – work for a larger one, in order to learn more about performing that kind of 'big business'. The final basis of power, **expert power**, bears the least relevance to business contexts. It concerns the value of publicly approved forms of expertise – for example, the fact that a medical degree and surgical fellowship are widely considered to be an adequate basis for performing an operation on another human being.

This typology has been consistently and productively applied within the marketing channels literature in the 1970s and 1980s. **Marketing channels** refer to chain-like relationships through which business progresses. Within traditional product industries, this often starts with suppliers, and continues on to manufacturers, distributors, and then parties who interface with consumers (retailers, salespeople, etc.). Over time, a handful of marketing scholars achieved great success using political analysis to understand the inherently political nature of these channels (e.g. Gaski and Nevin, 1985; Gaski, 1984; Hunt and Nevin, 1974; El-Ansary and Stern, 1972). These relationships can be highly political, as gaining power over either upward or downward partners can increase the returns to an actor. Historically, suppliers have often tried to hijack distribution chains by threatening to withhold supply, or by gaining a crucial monopoly which only they can deliver (e.g. being the only producer of a certain leather required for a particular model of shoe).

Over time, however, we have seen a rise of power among traders and retailers. Firms such as Wal-Mart have massive global operations, and they often use volume arguments to demand lower prices for goods. Larger grocers such as Tesco have come under fire for entering into exclusive, high-volume contracts with suppliers like farmers, only to later demand lower and lower prices for the continuation of the relationship (England, 2017; Butler, 2016; Moulds, 2015; Butler, 2013). At that point, the farm is already producing far more than it can get rid of via other channels, and often it has made significant investments in scaling up, which must be repaid.

Often, maintaining the relationship, even if it is barely adequate or not even adequate, is the only good solution remaining. In cases such as these, where one business partner is absolutely essential to the success of an operation, they may use economic (rather than physical) threats to get what they need. While we often do not talk about this as coercion, this is exactly what it is, in political terms.

Such strategies are so typical as to almost be considered best practice, but the literature indicates that there are practical as well as ethical reasons why coercion is not desirable. In the marketing channels literature, it was seen that this sort of use of power led to very low satisfaction within the supply chain, often leading to the end of valuable relationships. It also tends to be very unpopular with customers, and has led to demonstrations against retailers who have used these tactics.

While one might say these are not huge downsides, in situations where there are always new customers and new farms, the research indicates that this is still not great business practice. **Transaction cost analysis**, for example, shows that recreating the same relationships afresh costs more than the equivalent amount of savings (summarised in Rindfleisch and Heide, 1997).

Institutional Theory

Institutional theory sits on the precipice of not only political theory but also **social theory** – the study of society. As noted by DiMaggio and Powell (2012), **institutional theory** is interested in social structures, their permanence, and their authority. The idea here is that some phenomena are only *meaningfully* understood at an institutional level of analysis. For example, institutional theory researchers argue that consumer research that only looks at the individual level of analysis is incomplete, as it does not attend to the larger social structures which largely dictate how individuals behave. An example can be found when one tries to understand an individual's fashion sense, which will likely be best understood as originating from larger subcultures, national cultures, and market environments, rather than solely from an individual's imagination.

In doing this sort of analysis, these founders of the field and their many adherents find it valuable to consider how routines, rules, and norms – produced intentionally or unintentionally – become authoritative and largely guide how people act in a variety of situations. Just stating a rule, even unthinkingly, tends to create an expectation among most individuals that they should follow it. Taken together, Badiou's theory of ethics would be commensurable with an institutional theory approach to society, as both see an individual's views as largely dictated by the environment in which they operate.

Before moving further, it may be helpful to be explicit about what institutions are. An **institution** can be as small as a single organisation and its many stakeholders (for example, a university, all those it employs, its students, its neighbours, the broader society it serves). That said, more often than not institutional theory scholars study larger institutions such as 'fashion', 'global fashion', or 'the London fashion design scene'. The term **institutional field** can be used to describe the entire collection of actors who are affected and as such must be considered.

Scott (2001) finds that there are a handful of resources that are particularly valuable in institutional fields – beyond pure economic capital. The first, **regulatory legitimacy**, exists when an organisation follows the law. The second, **normative legitimacy**, occurs when it is considered to be 'behaving well', whether or not there are laws in place governing it. In many industries, for example, firms self-regulate in response to consumer concerns that there are no relevant laws in place to ensure legitimacy. The final element, **cultural-cognitive legitimacy**, considers whether behaviour encouraged by a firm 'makes sense' within a culture.

To make sense of this theory and its great value, it may be helpful to consider how it was previously used in marketing. Ashlee Humphreys (2010) applied this theory to the institution of casino gambling in America. There, she found that casinos were seen as law-breaking, undisciplined, and culturally uncool; in other words, they lacked all three of the forms of legitimacy noted above. Casinos managed to change this image by following the law, even requesting legislation where it did not exist; by self-regulating and paying taxes, where following the law was not seen as an adequate marker of discipline; and by securing the place of casinos in film, television, and tourist media to make it appear as a 'family friendly' activity.

Another powerful demonstration of the value of institutional theory can be seen in the work of Scaraboto and Fischer (2013). These authors were interested in the question of why mainstream designers and retailers in developed countries avoid producing clothes for larger people. Indeed, most fashion firms produce clothes in a very limited range of sizes, such that many completely healthy people will 'age out' of their lines over the course of a lifetime. They find that this is exactly the rationale of the designers – that thinness is a form of class-stratified exclusivity, and in order to defend the class-based arguments of elite cultural value, they are in fact invested in excluding particular groups of individuals. What is particularly interesting to see is that there is a movement of 'fat fashion' activists who had been engaging in massive, concerted efforts to raise awareness of this issue. Many were wealthy and personally pledged to spend great deals of cash if larger-sized goods were made. Even so, it is interesting to see that particular cultural commitments outweighed even economic incentives. That said, this stance could be seen as a sort of 'long game' – the designers could be thinking that being more inclusive would erode their brand in a way that is even worse for the bottom line over time.

Critical Discourse Analysis of Advertising

Critical discourse analysis is a remarkably flexible method which has near-infinite uses, from everyday life to the boardroom. I discuss a few examples here, and consider some reverberations in international practice.

To begin, critical discourse analysis can be used to understand the sorts of arguments that are being made by competitors. As noted in key texts on advertising analysis (Leiss et al., 2018; Hackley and Hackley, 2017), it is only through learning the language used within industries, among competitors, and by consumers that firms can achieve their goals. With this in mind, studying the ads of others, even in unrelated industries but similar markets, is best practice for ensuring interventions that will succeed.

In those key texts, as well as formal works on critical discourse analysis (Fairclough, 2014, 2003), it is noted that discourse does not refer only to words. Images, too, are a part of the language by which we communicate. Of course we are well aware of how images are used in advertising to 'say' that which might be too crass in words. An elegant dinner situation, for example, may be used to indicate wealth. Hey, it is better than simply screaming it! A more subtle notion, however, is the fact that advertising is just one of many 'visual discourses' afoot within business contexts today. As noted by Barthes (1967), fashion functions as a complicated language by which consumers are attempting to make statements about themselves. Inattention to issues of visual rhetoric and visual communication has grave implications within the world of marketing. We are all aware of ad campaigns that fell flat by attempting to reach us, but not capturing the appropriate style or conveying what was deemed inappropriate, for example the recent Pepsi ad featuring Kendall Jenner which co-opted the Black Lives Matter movement to help sell the sugary drink.

Finally, discourse analysis has been used extensively by scholars engaged in **advertising critique**, or advocating for **media literacy**. The goal of such work is to decode the language that marketers have been using, so that consumers can make a more informed decision about whether to make a particular purchase, or support a political party. Media literacy is considered to be an essential skill for successful navigation of the communication-heavy worlds of marketing in which we now live, with arguments that it should be an essential feature of school curricula (Mihalidis, 2018, 2014; Buckingham, 2003). At the same time, powerful individuals have often fought such measures forcefully. In the case of Italy, president Berlusconi was accused of having too much ownership of media, which could be used for not only political ends but also commercial and cultural ones (Ravi, 2017). Marketers, as a specific elite group, have often tried to maintain control of media literacy programmes or have even fought to defuse them, as they know that the general public would be less interested in buying what is sold, if they knew its true value (Eagle and Dahl, 2015).

Politics as We Know It: Government and Economy in the International Environment

I would be remiss not to mention 'politics as we know it', in a chapter on politics. There are undoubtedly implications of party politics, parliamentary politics, conservative politics, and leftist politics, within the world of international marketing. I discuss some key theories and ideas here.

On the one hand, we have the classic tension between capitalism, which favours the interests of property owners, and communism, which stresses the importance of labourers and everyday citizens (carers, the disabled, the elderly, etc.). As seen in Chapter 1, we exist in a post-political world, where the politics of capitalism is often 'the only game in town'. Still, there are no purely capitalist nations in the world even at present, and as such all involve some blending of public and private administration. We also have seen the emergence of new forms of capitalism in Russia and China, as they seek to join the game and yet also retain some features from the era of command economies. For businesses, it is essential to understand the pulse of government as it relates to one's enterprise, and these matters are only complicated when one is dealing with foreign governments.

Within political theory, there is a vibrant tradition concerning the **politics of consumption**. As noted in Chapter 2, the critical theory camp exemplified by the Frankfurt School was sceptical of popular culture and popular consumption, finding that consumer products may carry strong messages about conformity to pro-business interests. Consumerism as an institution, meanwhile, was argued to keep individuals working harder than they might otherwise want to. Postmodern scholars contested these notions to some degree, arguing that individuals often are capable of 'counter-readings' (a notion from Hall, 1997), which decode these meanings and repurpose them for alternative uses. Ultimately, this tradition has sided with a balanced approach informed by contemporary political philosophers such as Badiou. Here, it is argued that popular culture itself is not the problem, so much as its use for profit, and the massive amounts of ignorance surrounding these matters. Within international contexts, these issues are only starker, as grounds for deception are often greater between powerful multinational corporations, and customers who are often greatly lacking in experience with marketing communications.

Bringing it Together: SWOT and Five Forces Reconsidered – Marketing as Political

The cases above have all considered the ways in which marketing has used politics. But how is marketing, as a whole, political? A good way of understanding this matter is to look at the marketing strategy literature, and to understand how marketing is basically a political game.

Here, I focus specifically on the SWOT and Five Forces models. While these have not been theorised explicitly in terms of politics, one can easily see that they can be better understood by thinking of them politically. They are also relevant to students of international marketing, as there is nothing specifically domestic about these models. If anything, they created space for international considerations within the mainstream of marketing academia, and they also alerted domestic marketers to the fact that similar forces may be at play within their own contexts.

To start, SWOT is the model that asks us to think of the Strengths, Weaknesses, Opportunities and Threats facing any business – international or otherwise (Menon, 1999; Eisenhardt and Bourgeois, 1988). The first two aspects (the 'S' and the 'O') refer to matters internal to the firm. Strengths of course refer to the power the organisation possesses – the resources it has, and things it can do with those resources. Weaknesses, meanwhile, refer to any criteria upon which a firm is relatively disadvantaged. The 'O' and 'T' take into account the relationship between the firm and the external environment – in other words, they describe *political situations* and *political relationships*. Opportunities exist where a firm has unique abilities, compared to others, and threats of course exist where other actors (be they organisations, governments, or even consumer groups) have power over the firm.

Porter's Five Forces model, meanwhile, focuses on the power of customers, the power of suppliers, the threat of market entry, the threat from substitutes, and the intensity of rivalry within a market environment (Porter, 2008, 1979). That's a whole lot of power! While Porter does not conceptualise this model as specifically political, we must be reminded that where we see 'power', this does mean something political is afoot. Regardless of phrasing, this was a key intervention, as it encouraged marketers to think beyond the narrow confines of their own businesses, and unrealistic fantasies of what their businesses can do. Instead, marketers are encouraged to think strategically of what they can do that is likely to succeed.

While these models are valuable in their own right, there is good reason to understand specifically their political nature. First, we end up with a deeper, more theoretical understanding of what these models are. Next time you are in a board meeting and someone asks you to talk about the 'threat of new entrants', you will be able to say exactly what a threat is, and whether or not its size/magnitude/value is greater than your firm's own power. Even if you do work in domestic marketing, meanwhile, the market monitoring activities required to constantly be aware of the surrounding environment are of value to all businesses.

Second, and building upon this, we can make connections to other forms of political theory and political analysis. Critical discourse analysis, for example, could be used to compare strategy statements between two organisations. Elsewhere, political theory's emphasis on the role of governments reveals matters that businesses often overlook or downplay, but which are equally important to their success. Ultimately, it is having a realistic account of the power of all relevant actors – even those beyond a business and its customers – that will yield the best practice.

In the next section, we will look more deeply into this notion of marketing as a political game. There, I will focus specifically on models and theories within the international marketing literature – regardless of whether or not they used politics – and reconsider them in terms of this and our other two foundations (history and ethics). Chapter 4 will look specifically at the international marketing strategy literature, while Chapter 5 will consider consumer behaviour and research.

The Final Word: International Marketing as a Political Game

While the above is a great starting point – and one which I wish was used more in marketing – there is further work to be done to understand how this relates to international marketing. While SWOT and Five Forces can account for many of the major issues in international marketing, there are still many matters which are better understood through other concepts and theories. Indeed, that is what the remaining chapters of the book will explore! In preparation for all of that, let's identify a few dimensions specific to international marketing which merit consideration here.

To begin, we live in an ever-changing, increasingly integrated world economic system. To begin, literatures such as those on marketing channels and transaction cost analysis would do well to be updated, taking the contemporary business context into account properly. This research, especially where it considers polite ethics and the benefits of cooperation, was often done within single cultural contexts. With globalisation, we have seen the expansion of channel relationships across huge distances – and here I refer to political and cultural distance, as well as physical distance.

The core assumptions, including that such gaps are ripe for abuse, still hold. What *has* changed is that pursuing such disparities in chain relationships is now considered to be advisable, and the potential ethical implications have been radically discounted. Within garment manufacturing, for example, it is absolutely standard practice to open factories, *reduce* employees' wages, and then leave when unrest develops (Saxena, 2014; Rahman, 2013; Parenti, 2011). Taking on board examples like this, plus what we know about history and the international political environment, we see that much has been done to ensure that the most powerful parties within chain relationships can gain as much as possible with the least risk and cost.

Changes to channel relationships have only accelerated with neoliberalism, which has led to the deregulation of business, giving firms greater discretion concerning the conduct of contracts. In countries such as the UK and US, there is now little legislation to prevent businesses from signing any contract they like – and as such, there is no disincentive for powerful partners to constantly erode the return for other units which are dependent upon them. Tacit (unspoken) collusion has also become commonplace within many industries, such that all major players agree to use coercive contracts, thereby obliterating the weaker parties' chances of obtaining better contract terms.

We can see how this is harmful not only within relatively disadvantaged, developing world contexts, but also in the developed world as low-cost options from elsewhere put new pressures on domestic workers and businesses. In fact, the vantage point of international marketing raises questions about whether there is any such thing as a domestic business anymore, and reveals the importance of studying the wider political context for almost any venture. By studying topics like this, international marketing researchers could trickle up knowledge, changing our understanding of marketing more generally.

At the same time, the international environment also presents new opportunities. Though frequently downplayed, powerful firms from the 'global centre' often need information on local markets that can only be provided through local expertise. In this way, business partners who historically might have been considered to be weak can argue they have valuable information-based power, and use this to their advantage in negotiations. Market and consumer research is a key site for such arguments, as complicated local matters of culture and language may not be comprehensible without insider knowledge.

Institutional theory, too, is readily applicable to international contexts. This is because the work of launching a product in a foreign country or culture is largely a matter of learning the rules of legitimacy in unfamiliar territory. As in the case of Scaraboto and Fischer (2013), moreover, we see that it is often a complicated game of acquiring the right combination of both cultural and economic resources. Ultimately, some ventures will fail regardless of the investments made, as a result of strict local definitions of what is right and wrong business or cultural practice.

A key case for the importance of careful discourse development can be found within Palmer's aforementioned work on the marketing of formula milk internationally (Palmer, 2009). Poorly produced advertising and packaging has led to tragedy in many contexts. For example, a number of babies died in Laos, where Nestlé had been marketing both formula and creamer. To locals, the imagery on the creamer looked like a mother bear breastfeeding a baby, and in several cases was mistakenly used as such. Without resorting to such drastic examples, every mainstream international marketing textbook is rife with examples of international marketing failures, which occur on the grounds of poor presentation.

Another potential intersection of international marketing and the study of discourse can be seen in studies of development. There, we see a flourishing tradition of literature which has examined the often insulting language that NGOs and governments have used to justify aid and development projects. Clearly ignorant of the history revealed in Chapter 1, these organisations have often contended that the reason why poverty exists is that some cultures, nations, and even individuals are less capable than others – despite ample evidence to the contrary. One study of development discourse within African aid programmes came to much the same conclusions as Parenti – that Africa specifically has not been underdeveloped but overexploited, given that more wealth is removed from the continent (via labour and raw materials) than is returned via trade and aid. Here, it would be very valuable to see significantly more work on the role of marketing communications within developing contexts, as they may make similar claims, and function as part of the overall legitimation of unequal trade relationships.

Taken together, we see real implications of 'politics as we know it', as well as the politics of channels, firms, and communications, which are specific to the international environment.

PART II

Rethinking Practices

The 'New Foundations' chapters in Part I gave us an account of the historical emergence of international marketing, and a handful of starting points for pushing the discipline further. The mission of Part II is to really drill into the implications of this foundation for a wide range of discussions within the field.

Given the title and whatever marketing copy has been written for this book, you might have imagined that all of the chapters would be doing this. You'd be right too, because they do to a certain degree. Still, this section is the real heart of the project – the place where we get down to the nitty gritty, and really take apart existing thought on international marketing.

In bringing these fields together, I chose to organise Part II around three of the biggest, most impactful areas of international marketing research: that of marketing management, consumer behaviour, and intercultural marketing.I explain the rationale for this here. The only major area I can say is not represented is that of global marketing, and that is for good reason – de Mooij (2019) has already provided a damning critique of just how rare global marketing is. Basically, de Mooij notes that almost no firm is truly global (operating everywhere), so most are just some permutation of international. There are huge differences between 'global' firms. Finally, and perhaps most importantly, global strategies are so rare and unusual that they are better treated as a special case – and one that you will probably never have the need to implement – rather than as a foundation for a wide range of firms to consider.

This isn't to say that this book loses sight of the global context – indeed, I do anything but! Throughout, I have worked to integrate a world systems perspective, which is nothing if not an explanation of global interconnectedness. So rather than teaching you global marketing strategies that rarely exist in practice, I aspire instead to teach you why a **global mentality** is important even if you end up doing domestic marketing only!

It is important to note at this point that Chapters 4 and 5 tend to draw upon traditional (domestic) strategy and consumer behaviour at times. This is done intentionally, and is motivated by the fact that sometimes these are the most appropriate points of reference – the most informative ones, which have not suffered the 'double trickle down' into the depths of the international marketing literature. Where this is done, I work to 'internationalise' domestic-focused theory, as well as bring it into conversation with the foundations from Part I.

Intercultural marketing is less of a 'trickle down of a trickle down', so here we consider key principles from various cultural disciplines – specifically, cultural studies, cultural sociology, and cultural anthropology. Whoa, that's a whole lot of culture! While this field is arguably more closely related to its parent disciplines, I find that there are still many valuable and advanced topics that have yet to be integrated thoroughly into international marketing. This chapter uses these to add even more depth to this excellent and intriguing approach.

After all that, you should hang on for Part III on 'Envisioning Futures'. It's for your own benefit, as these chapters discuss two crucial contexts which may change international marketing entirely! There we will seek to build these challenges into the new model of international marketing which emerges here. In the section below, I will give a bit more detail on the chapters, and how they are all meant to come together.

Chapter 4 discusses what would traditionally be described as the fields of marketing strategy and management – basically, the part of our thought dedicated to what firms are actually doing, or at least thinking they are doing, or hoping they will do. From our new perspective, we see a critical, dispassionate view of what many of these activities really are. At the same time, we consider how difficult it would be to change the system through a brief consideration of business cases which addressed Marks & Spencer's anti-offshoring efforts.

Chapter 5 turns our attention to consumer research. This is a bit of a strange field. Some of its members are devoted to protecting consumer welfare, while others want to understand people so as to exploit them more effectively. Here, I begin by critically assessing what it means to be a consumer in general, and especially given the global geopolitical conditions revealed in Part I. From this new vantage point, I then reconsider some key models within the field. The chapter also features a case study on how even those in developing countries are being brought into the world economy, and developed as consumers.

Chapter 6 takes intercultural marketing to the next level. Not only do we revisit classic principles from cultural disciplines, but we also delve into a variety of advanced topics which have not historically been well integrated into international marketing discourse. It is truly unfortunate that this hasn't been done before, because (as you will see!) these are some of the most central and crucial questions within international marketing practice!!! One case in this section is that of the mass marketing of Mexican food by American firms. Here, I draw on the work of Jeffrey Pilcher and update it, to consider recent developments within the Trump era. Oh my... Another case considers the mass marketing of 'Scandi' design internationally.

Ultimately, there is no one way to approach international marketing practice. All three areas discussed in Part II are basics, which belong in any international marketing curriculum, and an education is only complete when we have access to all of them. View this part as a toolbox from which you can pick and choose as you need. At the same time, an argument can be made that we should always draw on all three of these wells of knowledge. There is no reason for a marketing strategy person to forget to consider consumer issues for example, and intercultural considerations really deserve to be integrated throughout! Indeed, one could argue that it is most ethical to do so, as anything less would ignore key stakeholders.

4

International Strategy, Reconsidered

Clarifying the Meaning of Common Practices

As noted in the Introduction, traditional international marketing textbooks have often sold us simplistic stories about this area of business practice. They might as well be labelled like any other consumer product, with bright labels and unbelievable slogans. 'You, *too*, can use the same strategies as Apple!'

Can We? Really?

This chapter seeks to reconceptualise the nature of international marketing strategy, based on the foundations we're learned in Part I. It's a big task, but it's a valuable one. Without a more realistic, analytically useful sense of how it is done, our knowledge of this area of business practice suffers.

We should also be reminded of the history through which marketing as we know it developed – specifically, that it thrives and usually even depends upon the unequal division of labour and wealth. It benefits from situations where workers and consumers lack information, media literacy, and the power to regulate. While many marketing books refer to this form of business practice as a set of benevolent exchanges between buyers, sellers, and workers, we must note that the greatest value tends to be created from exploiting divisions between sellers and all others.

While these divisions exist domestically, they tend to be even deeper internationally, increasing the potential for value creation significantly. This may seem like great news to some businesspeople, but it is not great news to the customers who are in the weaker position. And while we may feel that we are 'the bosses' in our work, we must remember that in relation to all other firms, we are the *customers*. Whatever manipulative things we are doing in our own practice will ultimately be done to us as well.

Recent philosophical developments raise some questions about just how much power is held not only by individuals, but even for example by a business. At the end of the chapter, we'll consider the case of British retail giant Marks & Spencer, which went from being a powerful market leader to a follower of fast-fashion shops. Here, we see a real example of the sort of negotiations of power which exist in marketplaces. Taken together, the chapter is organised around two principles:

> Principle 4a: While internationalisation is often considered inherently valuable as it can increase economy of scale, it is not a guaranteed route to profitability. It depends on the context, resources, and strategies of the firm.

> Principle 4b: The most powerful players within a set of interconnected international marketers generally set the terms by which everyone else must play.

As a very small preview: we are left with some serious doubts about whether we can all be just like Apple. To start, we do not have a time machine and cannot go back to the beginning of home computing, placing ourselves in the ideal technology development location in the world. That's one problem...

What Is 'International Business'?

In order to re-evaluate how international marketing strategy really works, we need to begin by reconsidering its role within larger international businesses (or organisations, in the case of non-profits).

Perhaps resulting from the homogeneity of conceptualisations of international marketing in the past literature, students frequently believe that international marketing and global business are one and the same. As noted in the introduction, this is not the case. While global business is an important site of international marketing activity, it is only one such site. Moreover, what counts as global can vary greatly by product category. Louis Vuitton, for example, may consider itself a global luxury marketer, but the actual number of countries where they can operate is likely to be quite low. Unilever, meanwhile, can operate in quite a large number of countries because commodity-grade shampoo and ice cream are (relatively) more accessible products.

Building on Chapter 1, it should be noted here that there is no one 'right' or 'wrong' size or model of international business. Great profits may be reaped from many unglamorous professions such as **whole-saling**, **shipping** and **logistics**. These topics receive short shrift in the usual textbooks, and where they are covered it is dead boring. All said, the nameless intermediaries of our economy often take home huge sums. Given that they work in a business-to-business capacity, this sort of work often offers the opportunity to remain nameless and hidden from the general public... in other words, it's a perfect recipe for engaging in nefarious behaviour, uncontested, with little to no chance of protest. Hey, what could go wrong with that?!

Don't believe me? Feel free to pick up a copy of Levinson's work on the history of the shipping container (Levinson, 2016), which goes into great detail about the tremendous volume of commerce conducted by water to this date. Most of the things we own have come off such a ship, and yet we know very little about them... for example, the fact that they tend to use the most terrible, leftover fuel and are an environmental nightmare (Gabbatiss, 2018).

Small and medium sized enterprises may also be perfectly profitable – even reaping greater margins than global businesses. What needs to be taken into account is that the larger the operation, the greater its *costs*, as well as the **economy of scale**. Working for Google, Apple or Nike does not necessarily mean that you will make the most money... unless you are the CEO. Indeed, the vast majority of people who work for such a firm may make very little, and could do better and enjoy greater **leadership** opportunities elsewhere.

A key question here is that of **organisation** – what are the **boundaries** of the international operation? Does the firm do its own shipping and distribution, or does it rely on existing companies and retailers? Is customer service **in-house** or **outsourced**? International business involves not only the channel relationships discussed in Chapter 3, but also a great many horizontal relationships, and the firm must decide which are done in-house and out-of-house.

The business-to-business parts of a business, in particular, are a key site where international exchanges occur. Take, for instance, a distinctly British firm such as Sainsbury's. While the products on the shelf may carry consistent store branding, and the shops may feature a number of British brands, Sainsbury's must interface with a great many international partners in reaching this state. Like the discussion of interdependence of world commodities markets in Chapter 1, this international exchange similarly raises questions about what is even domestic anymore. From cases like this we see why international marketing can have relevance, no matter what work you go into.

Baack et al. (2018) provide some fairly interesting food for thought about the boundaries and choices of your business. They refer to four key models of international business. The first is the **ethnocentric** business, wherein all major decision-making occurs within a single country. The returns from the business, too, tend to be channelled back to the home country for tax purposes, and as much as possible, individuals from that country or culture are 'sent out' into international markets. The term 'ethnocentric' has negative connotations, and the authors do not seem to be avoiding those potential associations. In other words, their choice of this terminology is a way of tacitly stating that this can often be a foolish, bull-headed approach as it is unlikely that a team from a single country will have the adequate expertise for successfully pulling off an international campaign that will be seen as legitimate – or even one that will be capable of profit (even if not liked locally).

The other three models can generally be seen as different permutations of the same idea: that governance should be more diffuse. The first, and most standard from previous business practice, is the **regiocentric**. Regiocentric organisations have different regional headquarters. This is argued to reduce the physical and cultural distance between the appropriate centre and its customers. That said, regiocentric business strategy can suffer from many of the pitfalls of ethnocentric organisation – though on a slightly smaller scale. Regional classifications such as 'East Asia', for example, are a bit ridiculous given the diversity and sheer size of the region. Countries like Japan, Thailand, South Korea, and China have radically different cultures, languages, economic systems, and legal systems. While regional managers may find it somewhat easier to work on such a scale, given that physical proximity means that there is a longer history of trade between the countries, there is still so much work to be done to ensure success. Having national headquarters in each country of operations could be seen as one form of regiocentric operation; at least in this case, one would be dealing with one legal system, and a predominant national culture (though there may still be many different subcultures or languages, even within a country).

Polycentric organisations have multiple centres, often defined in terms of national headquarters. That said, other forms of geographic organisation are possible as well. Google, for example, has numerous centres within the United States, but only one in some countries. In some versions of polycentric organisation you see accountability and power equally distributed across units – a divergence from the hierarchical (and hence potentially exploitative) form of ethnocentric business. Firms become **geocentric** when they let go of the idea of a 'home country' entirely, seeing power as equally distributed across all of the outposts.

A key question here is what sort of **staffing** issues you see related to your venture. Do you need **local knowledge**, and if so, how will you get it?

Do local actors provide enough input that they should be equal (or otherwise powerful) partners, or can they be treated as expendable? Are they full-time staff who identify with your firm, or do you hire contractors and one-off services? Do they benefit from the security and benefits that come with working in your home country? Do you contribute tax revenue locally, thus helping the societies in which you operate as well as your own? At the end of the day, one must decide what the value of the world's knowledge is to you. It is often essential to success and as such is largely the source of value, but there are no regulations that enforce like-for-like compensation, and many international businesses treat knowledge as if it is infinitely replaceable.

Mergers and acquisitions are an almost canonical form of international marketing practice, which merits mention here as well as anywhere else, given that it concerns the structure of a business. This occurs when a firm takes control or otherwise integrates partners. When this occurs within a channel between adjacent links, this is **vertical integration**. Whether or not this is advisable is, like anything in business, largely context dependent. Taking over retail operations in a foreign country, for example, may be more trouble than it is worth. At the same time, the greater the scope of the organisation brought under a single centre (in terms of taxation, management, etc.) the greater the value that those stakeholders can keep for themselves. Taking over operations in other countries is often a way in which firms can increase the return that is available to that particular group – even if it is no more efficient.

Finally, it should be noted that vertical integration is sometimes performed to neutralise a threat within the supply chain. **Horizontal integration** may occur when a firm uses its expertise in a given area to acquire an operation at the periphery of its usual remit. A fast food restaurant may acquire a coffee chain, for example. This may also be a way of neutralising threats, as it ensures that customers have fewer choices – and as such, more revenue is returned to a single organisation. Either form of integration may be used to purchase local knowledge, making it one's own.

Here, I contend that decisions about the boundaries and organisation of a firm are actually big philosophical questions. To begin, they ask us to think about what type of business we have, and what it is meant to do. They say much about the **values** of an organisation, which in turn have an ethical component. Having options to organise a business in one's interests indicates a great deal of power and consequently responsibility. You've got the upper hand if you can choose to be a large, centrally organised multinational which harvests value from customers and workers throughout the world. At the same time, you could yield some of that power and control to others as an ethical choice. Sometimes this is even the more financially sensible option! Whatever your feelings on these matters, one thing is for certain: these are foundational questions which must be satisfactorily settled before starting a new business or strategy.

Overall Strategy: Drivers of Internationalisation

International marketing textbooks and guides note that there are a variety of forces which largely encourage **internationalisation** (the decision to work in more than one country). Some may be **internal** to the organisation, and relate to the expertise or desires of the staff. In the case of innovations with universal value (e.g. medical devices and pharmaceuticals), there is inherent value to bringing the product to as many people as possible.

Much of the time, however, the reason for internationalising is external to the organisation – sometimes referred to as **external drivers of internationalisation**. While there are many ways to present them, the **PESTLE** model of international business is as good as any (see Czinkota et al., 2011 as well as Baack et al., 2018 for more information). This model is used to help firms understand at a *macro* environmental level what unique competitive advantage they may have, within the international context of their given industry.

The first element of the PESTLE model is the political, and refers to governmental matters. Trade bloc integration or disintegration (which many hope will happen as they advocate for Brexit) are forces that may affect whether a firm seeks to achieve its goals internationally or domestically. E refers to economic factors, and includes differences in currencies and about value. S stands for sociocultural matters. T refers to technological factors, for example the fact that a country has some particularly efficient and valuable form of manufacturing. L refers to legal concerns and differences in regulations. A negative case of using legal opportunities to internationalise can be found in cigarette companies' decisions to ramp up their marketing initiatives internationally, once the health consequences of smoking became well known within the EU, Canada, and the United States. E refers to the environment, and this means industrial challenges, more than the natural environment (like sustainability). This is often the deciding factor, as companies realise that they are so efficient or well resourced that they could outperform local firms. Ultimately, choices about what internationalisation means are often described in terms of 'country selection and market entry', which biases decision-making towards legal and political definitions of the challenge of international marketing. Here, we should be reminded of Usunier and Lee's (2013) critique, that international marketing is so often a matter of intercultural work. Successfully negotiating cultural differences among staff, throughout channels and with consumers is often the more difficult work, and it is also activity which makes up the 'day to day' of many international marketers' careers.

Pricing Strategies

Pricing is one of the most foundational aspects of marketing – so much so that it merited being canonised as one of McCarthy and Kotler's '4 Ps' (alongside Place, Product and Promotion; see Kotler and Armstrong, 2017). Many marketing researchers and scholars forget just how important it is, assuming that key pricing decisions are just maths. All said, pricing is one of the most controversial points of marketing practice, and this only becomes more pronounced in the case of international marketing.

As noted in Chapter 2, Plato had a good point, which modern marketing has now forgotten. As a refresher, he argued that charging two prices for the same product is unethical, as it should have only one 'value'. Again, within modern marketing, charging two prices for a product is so uncontroversial as to have a name: **price discrimination**. Marketers defend the practice, arguing that products have different value to different customers. Moreover, they view marketing as a 'service', which gives consumers products where they want them, when they want them, with the argument that products differ in terms of how they are distributed. In other words, price differences are explained as 'value added'. Meanwhile, Aristotle raised questions about how shopkeepers and traders (intermediaries and end links in supply chains, in modern parlance) exploit their power, using it to charge great sums for products and not sharing that money adequately with producers.

Within international marketing, the topic of pricing is particularly heated – so much so that it is often discussed in the rare sections on 'unethical practice' within standard textbooks. To begin, there is a long history of price discrimination across geographic markets. First world customers are often charged enormous sums for goods that were made cheaply. A recent example of outrage on such an issue can be seen in the case of eyewear, with angry consumers turning to firms like Zenni, which can offer developing world prices – or at least a point in between that and developed world standards – for a product. Perhaps more troubling, however, is that prices are often set very unfairly within developing countries. As noted by Baack et al. (2018), setting prices based on local standards of acceptability is best practice... but this is often not what is done. More commonly, businesses determine prices of an internationalisation based on their own break even or profitability measurements, then introduce and heavily promote products regardless of whether or not they are affordable. In some contexts, this simply backfires and the marketer learns an important lesson. In many others, however, we see people in developing countries struggling to afford goods they have been absolutely convinced they need.

This matter is exacerbated when international firms acquire smaller, more local operations. Despite the fact that large multinationals are more efficient, and thus should be able to provide better prices, they often devote their efficiency to achieving a total monopoly, and then provide worse prices. The impact of such a strategy on local economies is of course tragic. Often we see jobs lost as operations (like marketing and distribution, and sometimes even production) are taken over or switched over to other providers. Tax money tends to flow out of the country. And then of course, your average consumer is also paying more for a good that could have been produced in a way that was better for their own economy.

How one feels about all of this depends again on the values of the business. Consider the **stakeholder theory of the firm** (see Freeman, 1994 for more information). Stakeholders include all groups affected by the organisation, like customers, communities, employees, and the natural environment – as well as shareholders and investors. While generally considered to encourage more expansive ethical thinking than a solely firm-based perspective, stakeholder theory encounters difficulties within some legal contexts. In the United States, for example, firms are obligated by law to put shareholders' interests before those of any other stakeholders (*Santa Clara County* v. *Southern Pacific Railroad Co.* (1886) 118 U.S. 394). Some scholars say that this case gave corporations **personhood**, in that they were then allowed to enter into contracts and dealings in the same way a person might; at the same time, it is a controversial notion as it is very hard to imprison a company! This brings with it the critique that American firms have all of the opportunities of individuals with little of the actual responsibilities (Clements, 2014). While this may sound like an obscure matter of only domestic relevance, it is in fact foundational to the entire world economy. By being free of ethical obligations which firms face in other countries, American firms can often offer their goods and services at a lower price. This can make it difficult, if not impossible, for firms to compete. Firms interested in more ethical practice, in countries where that is better protected by law, may find that they cannot engage in their ethical practice anyway because it makes them uncompetitive. In short, the United States becomes the lowest common denominator from which the rest of the world must follow.

In closing this discussion of how one distributes wealth generated from pricing among one's stakeholders, I must raise a critique of my own concerning corporate personhood. While nominally plausible, it is dubious under further examination as almost all businesses make *some* allowance for non-economic value production. Take the case of a hotel. There are many areas upon which it can cut corners, from the quality of sheets to the number of towels. Most corporate hotels do engage in some of these practices, but there is probably no hotel that engages in all possible practices of value minimisation. In short, corporate personhood is often cited when companies want to defend something seen as of questionable ethics, and it is often ignored at other times.

Valuation, Rather Than Pricing?

Taken together, the topic of pricing might be better thought of as **valuation** – the study of how value is attributed to products. Historically, valuation in marketing contexts has been guided by the assumptions of traditional economics – that 'markets decide willingness to pay', and as such, firms are simply doing what the market has told them to do. You know, a claim which absolves them of all responsibility.

Of course, a look at past marketing history reminds us that markets do not really decide. In addition to the past cases already explored, I will tell you one more – a favourite of mine. It concerns the introduction of avocados to Britain – a task which may not seem international, but given that avocados will never grow here, certainly is. There was no initial demand by British consumers for avocados. Really, who would want a new, unusual fruit/vegetable that they did not know how to prepare? Sainsbury's, however, saw a potential for profit regardless. They singlehandedly assumed responsibility for introducing British consumers to this product in the 1970s. Launching it successfully required in-store demonstrations to teach consumers how to use it, and to give a taste so they knew it was worth the risk. Strategies like this are shocking to classical and neoclassical economists, as they fundamentally should not work. This is exactly the contribution that marketing made to business practice, by arguing that it was possible – even advisable – to do things which economists thought of as 'socially useless'. The term for this strategy is called the creation of **primary demand** and is considered relatively unproblematic. Neoliberal economics has incorporated such ideas and legitimated them. At the same time, one should note that an ethical decision is nevertheless made – firms do decide that individuals need things in their lives that they do not actually need (Kotler and Armstrong, 2017).

We need to keep in mind that consumers trade not only in money but also in labour. Crucial here is the notion of **exchange**, as well as the historical foundations of unequal exchange. In short, valuation is the point at which the relative value of consumers' and workers' lives is weighed against the interests of firms. Firms are usually the ones that get to set the scales, so it is unsurprising that others are often short-changed.

It should be noted that money is not the only cost or way in which we pay for valuable market offerings. We will return to this issue in Chapter 7, where we consider how we trade **attention** (viewing ads) and **privacy** (allowing cookies and access to personal information) in exchange for things we want.

Special Topic in Valuation: Fair Trade

A topic of major interest within valuation is of course fair trade. **Fair trade** is a movement that seeks to provide living wages for producers, via a variety of schemes which may differ significantly in the actual compensation offered. Some allow local producers to engage in active negotiations of what is fair, while others (such as Sainsbury's new scheme, which diverges from existing international agreements) just set a price and say 'that's fair'. Fair trade products often have at least a small price premium, though in certain industries and contexts (tea and bananas in the UK, for example) they have become so commonplace that almost all products (including store brands and generic) are fair trade, and so consumers become immune to seeing the logo.

There are many interesting issues to consider here, as it is a special case of pricing. The first concerns the relationship between the premium, and the price given to farmers. Often, they are not synonymous, with companies keeping part of the added value (Sylla, 2014). There is certainly an ethical dilemma here! A second is to radically consider the definition of what are 'fair wages', even in contexts where workers have the opportunity to negotiate for higher repayment. Knowing what we know about history, we see that wages in these places have been consciously produced to be low, and that the justification for this historically was often quite dubious (e.g. involving theft, colonialism, racism, etc., as seen in Chapter 1). Some justice-oriented scholars urge for strategies which would gradually equilibrate wages across the world (Cope, 2015).

A third matter concerns whether industries care about being fair. Within the UK, a few are quite consistently concerned with the fairness of their trade practices, but the vast majority of product categories have no such discussion occurring in them at all. The lack of debate around fair trade in such areas is obviously a reason for concern. At the same time, considering why certain industries practise fair trade also raises problematic findings. If one looks closely, it can be seen that the goods most likely to fall under mass fair trade distribution are those that have been historically subject to imperialist injustices. They are sites where some of the worst abuses and labour contestations have occurred. On the one hand, their enshrinement of fair trade can be seen as part of a dark history, which continues into the present in that the wages even under these schemes are rarely very fair (would *you* like to live on the wages of people who pick your produce?). On the other hand, the fact that these protections have occurred in industries where workers have organised is encouraging, and raises a case for why labourers in other industries should also kick up a fight. A question that is often asked in my International Marketing classes is why there isn't a fair trade laptop. Good question! In the wake of the Foxconn scandal (Merchant, 2017), there is certainly adequate public awareness of issues within electronics production.

A final issue is the idea that fair trade products are highly expensive for good reason, and that in turn no one can afford them. Similar arguments are made about sustainable products, which I will discuss in Chapter 8. Here, the literature indicates that this is both realistic and unrealistic. On the one hand, fairer and more sustainable operations tend to be much smaller, and their costs of business tend to be much higher. They simply do not have the established business models and relationships that large, multinational corporations have. The actual cost of producing goods in a fairer way is often not so high (Alamgir and Banerjee, 2019). The price premium which would be required for large corporations to give true living wages to those who work in developing world factories is only £0.51 per item – nowhere near figures like £30, that many consumers would expect (Banerjee, 2017). Moreover, research has been done that shows that consumers would be willing to pay this premium – they would like to have ethical relationships with producers, if this is all that would be required – even in industries like fast fashion (think Primark, for example). In digging deeper, these researchers found that the large MNCs that contract with sweatshops are simply unwilling to part with that £0.51, which they easily could.

⬤⬤⬤⬤ International Finance

Finance is generally a part of the discipline of... finance... but it is covered regularly in marketing textbooks, as a basic understanding of its relationship to marketing activities is necessary. Within the international context, it is often discussed in dry terms, but this is yet another case where our past knowledge is reanimated with consideration of findings from the disciplines of history, politics, and ethics.

Finance differs from marketing in that it seeks to create value through the creative deployment of **money**. **Lending** is one of the most common forms of finance, and is of course predicated on offering money up-front, in return for the money plus **interest** at a later date. Of all of the business disciplines, it is the one that is the most indifferent to the needs and desires of other stakeholders, or even the most basic alternative goals of a firm. For example, while the hotel owners in the cases above are balancing a variety of interpersonal and aesthetic considerations in their decisions about what is an appropriate level of quality for a hotel, someone *financing* a hotel chain is primarily interested in how value can be maximised.

As such, banking and financial services are the typical industries for financial knowledge, but it is notable that finance as an industry has encroached on many others, often pushing standards further and further towards a pure financial logic. Anthropologist Karen Ho (2009) did well to illuminate this phenomenon, showing how New York investment banks have promoted this model widely and internationally, despite the fact that it is actually disastrous in many other contexts. In understanding how finance relates to international marketing, we must keep this fact – that finance has different priorities than marketing – in mind.

Put simply, finance stresses that money should go where it can be most profitably deployed. This is ultimately the foundation of much of the more unsavoury activity that occurs under the umbrella of international marketing. Firms enter international markets, destroy the local competition or take it over, and provide a product at perfectly fine margins. From a more balanced, multiple stakeholder perspective, which takes into account at least consumer interests as well as the firm's, there is no reason to leave. Those employing financial logic, however, often advocate leaving the international expansion when there is *any* more profitable use of the funds.

In short, financial logic has a tendency to be so dispassionate to even the most basic of human concerns that the famous documentary *The Corporation* (2003) found that businesspeople and firms which espouse these concerns would be considered to be psychopathic, within reigning definitions in psychiatry. At the same time, this financial logic is considered to be completely standard and legal within contemporary business practice – in cases such as the US, seen above, it may even be legally mandated to a certain degree.

Case in Point

Marks & Spencer's Complicated, Sophisticated Offshoring Policy

In understanding the relevance of these principles to an actual international marketing context, I find the case of Marks & Spencer to be particularly interesting.

Marks & Spencer views itself as a quintessentially British brand, that prides itself on selling the best British products available. It has an established base of loyal consumers who love the firm for this very reason. M&S did well with this strategy, becoming a cornerstone of the British retail scene and achieving occasional international expansions (mostly across Europe, but also with some expansions into the Middle East and East Asia). It did so well as to become the first British firm to have recorded profits over £1 billion, an achievement reached in 1998. At the same time, not much more than a year later, the firm was on the verge of bankruptcy, and had to engage in emergency measures to be solvent (*The Telegraph*, 2008). What happened?

One of the biggest factors is that this domestic business had become increasingly challenged by domestic competitors over the course of many years. Several academics have previously recounted this history, and their work is the foundation of the case presented here (Toms and Zhang, 2016; Abecassis-Moedas, 2007; Khan, 2005). The way that these competitors managed to somehow outdo a standard, successful strategy had to do with the international nature of their operations. In short, the crash of M&S occurred at the moment that the majority of other businesses chose to outsource their production. In doing so, they were able to reduce prices, and even where

(Continued)

(Continued)

deductions were modest, consumers went where the value was. M&S, meanwhile, had remained dedicated to their model of sourcing products domestically, as much as possible, which they thought was ultimately best for the national economy, and for those they employed here. Also, they knew that the value gained for firms and customers in internationalising was usually produced by making life harder for producers.

M&S made a very interesting and unique strategic decision, which can be understood in terms of the Badiouian ethical philosophy presented previously. They realised they were no longer in a position of power within their given industry. Whether or not they stayed in business was largely in the hands of their competitors and consumers, who wanted to make trades that were not in line with the firm's ethics. They considered what the market would be like if they exited entirely – but decided to maintain their organisational (and individual, in the case of employees) ethics and using good labour practices was the only way to go.

Unlike many who have decided to drop out along the way, giving up the life of the sell-out, they chose to stay open and in the industry – even if it meant lowering their ethical standards for some period of time. They maintained that this was not the ethical position of the organisation, and that they would work to reorganise and become more efficient, in the hope that they could eventually find a way to reach the standards they believed were best. Moreover, they contended that by maintaining their position as a major player within the British economy, they could have a say in government talks, industry discussions, and other sites where standards and regulation are debated.

In reading this case, I should note that advocating for the interesting, albeit complex position of a firm like M&S is *not* the same as advocating kneejerk economic nationalism. Moreover, it does not mean that a blinkered approach focused solely on developing one's domestic economy is best. International cooperation could be very valuable, so long as the economic wealth produced is more evenly shared.

The Final Word: International Marketing Via All Three Foundations

Traditional international marketing textbooks are careful to include some content about the ethics of international marketing, but the topic is often given short shrift. A handful of 'focus' sections, for example, will point out some particularly glaring examples of bad international marketing practice which has occurred in the past. These tend to be the sorts of examples that even colleagues within the international marketing community thought were suspect at the time.

We get a different result when we reconsider international marketing from an approach that takes ethics as a starting point. This perspective stresses the fact that power differentials are not simply incidental to international marketing practice, but often are the reason for internationalisation itself. In turn, this more honest focus helps us understand why international marketing is so tempting to students and practitioners alike.

On the one hand, much of the most successful and standard international marketing practice is problematised through this approach. Once one's eyes are opened, it is a bit terrifying just how little consideration such matters usually get within traditional textbooks, where the definition of 'bad practice' tends to be so narrow. Where we do see examples, they often focus on firms that broke regulations, as if law should be the only ethical standard by which we conduct our lives. Also as if law itself was not politically established!

This chapter also reminds us of why a deeper historical approach – like the one from Chapter 1 – is valuable. First, it allows us to understand where the standard practices of today came from. While we have often naturalised their political foundations, deeper investigation reveals that there is often much more at stake than is obvious from first glance. Second, looking to the past may give us some insight into what customers and even businesses may find unsavoury in the future. The international marketing books of 2040 will be looking for examples from today, so with that in mind, it is important to consider whether you are acting on the edge of acceptability – lest you find yourself in one of the maligned 'naughty corners' of even traditional textbooks! Wise firms with a long-term orientation will consider these issues now, rather than find themselves disbanded and liquidated.

The case of the tobacco industry is another example where we see difficult compromises that had to be made, as vaping was considered to be an easier way to phase out the industry than closing doors entirely, which would have financially destroyed employees and shareholders (Gostin and Glasner, 2014; Cahn and Siegel, 2011). On second thought, perhaps that is not the greatest example... maybe they could have just closed their doors...

In any case, compromises such as these, and that of M&S, are more often than not what ethical international marketing looks like in practice. Often, the stress-inducing challenge of 'doing good' is not even on the table, but we are reminded that 'doing better' may very well be.

5

The Global Orchestration of 'Consumer' 'Behaviour'

Consumer behaviour is the subdiscipline of marketing dedicated to developing knowledge about how we procure and use goods and services. Like marketing more generally, it emerged to address gaps within economic thought. The need was acute for those interested in consumer matters, as economics really leaves much to be desired on this particular subject. Even in this day and age, you can open an introductory microeconomics textbook and see that the foundational conceptualisation of consumption is that of **aggregate demand**. Such a concept asks that we treat customers as an anonymous, homogeneous group, which is preposterous in most real market contexts. Imagine an 'aggregate market for shoes' – as if there were only one style, brand and size!

In attempting to address the inanity of such a proposition, marketing researchers started by drawing upon the discipline of psychology. While this did facilitate a somewhat more sophisticated view of how markets actually work, it also introduced some new problems (see discussion by Askegaard and Linnet, 2011; Tadajewski, 2006). By thinking of consumption as a 'psychological matter', it implies that bad **decisions** and even plain bad **consumer outcomes** result from bad **cognition**. This implies that if only people were smarter, or more sane, then they would not be deceived or experience material poverty. Yikes!

Later scholars added some nuance by acknowledging that **emotion**, **situational factors** (like hunger) and **impulse** could also affect what we do. Sociocultural researchers then considered how family, cultures and subcultures exert **social influence** on our decisions. These are important contributions, and if you are learning about this subject for the first time, it certainly merits considering a standard text like Solomon et al. (2013). Still, I have always found something to be missing within them. I had been introduced to the subject at the age of 14, and it was the first thing I ever wanted to research; at the same time, getting the answers I wanted has been a *much* longer process than I had ever imagined!

You see, I had a very cool secondary school teacher who taught us about **conspicuous consumption** – the use of goods and services to convey social status. I thought *finally*, we were learning about a subject in school which had real, everyday value. It was something I could see in the world around me. Perhaps more importantly, it seemed like a problem that required attention, as I found many of my peers struggling to keep up with the ever-expanding expectations of fashion and cultural consumption. When I got to university I sought research assistantships with anyone who would help me learn about the topic. I looked first in economics, sociology, cultural studies, American studies, and political science as they were the sort of classes where I first learned about conspicuous consumption. While it is an established topic in those disciplines, it is somewhat niche, so at my university I had to look elsewhere for supervisors who would take on the topic. They were found in clinical psychology, quantitative psychology, and consumer behaviour – *in the business school*!

Here, I seek to put these pieces back together, putting some of the great material from history, politics and ethics (as well as from other disciplines!) into conversation with mainstream consumer behaviour theories. As noted by Askegaard and Linnet (2011), this is something the field of consumer research absolutely needs, as it is lacking in understanding of the macro-level context in which individual, group, and cultural behaviour occurs. The need only becomes more clear when considered in terms of the model of world economy introduced in Part I – New Foundations. Here, I argue that it is not helpful to think of consumption as individual behaviour so much as the outcome of a complicated, socio-historically determined process.

Building on this, the next section considers whether it is still useful to think of ourselves as 'consumers'. Here it is viewed as a real term which exists in the world, but also a problematic way to think of humanity. Later sections trace some concrete applications of this approach to consumption. Classic models of consumer behaviour (concerning needs and values, the diffusion of innovations, market research, and rationality) are then reconsidered in light of this new framework. The case study presents a critical discourse analysis of how individuals are produced as consumers within developing countries. The chapter concludes with a critical interrogation of the notion of consumer ethics, questioning both the notion that we have many real choices, and the injustices of the global stratification of consumer participation.

There are ultimately many reasons to study consumer behaviour, and many different ways you could use the knowledge provided here. The usual justification within international marketing textbooks is that it allows you to market more effectively. At times, this is couched in terms of the brutal pursuit of profit, but elsewhere the emphasis is on sensitivity to consumers. I take a different view of this matter, and always convey it to my students. It is important to note that whatever you do professionally in the future, this topic will have relevance to you as you will always be a consumer. Yes, even if you throw this book away, pick up a saw and become a carpenter.

With this in mind, you should think carefully about how you would plan to use the knowledge in this chapter. It can be tempting to take this realistic account of how consumer culture operates as a 'how-to' guide in the arts of consumer exploitation. Indeed, many students are eager to study the subject as they think they can master it, ensure that no firm ever fools them again, and make massive profits orchestrating their customers' behaviour. To this I can only say that… the degree to which you are eager to do this is generally correlated with your own consumer desires! If you think about it carefully, you will see that we tend to work in marketing in order to buy consumer goods that are marketed to us, which then allows those marketers to buy consumer goods and then… it is a cycle that can continue *ad infinitum*. Some say that the only way to win may actually be to get off the carousel entirely!

At the end of the chapter, it is my hope that you will see how your understanding of individual 'consumer' 'behaviours' is enhanced by integrating all of these perspectives into past approaches drawn from economics and psychology. Bringing this knowledge into your own life may be aided by considering the following principles:

Principle 5a: Our understanding of consumer culture can be improved by thinking of it as a system produced in specific times and places, for the purpose of maximising the production of wealth.

Principle 5b: 'Being a consumer' is best understood as an obligation produced by consumer culture, which makes individuals believe that they are personally responsible for their success (or failure) within this complicated political system.

Principle 5c: While international consumer research texts often urge careful consideration of local culture, a historical and political model reveals how many firms can avoid doing this work through brute force strategies such as establishing *de facto* monopolies, rather than winning customers by consent.

Principle 5d: The ethical and political dimensions of consumption are better conceptualised as collectively and sociologically determined rather than individual.

The Historical Emergence of Consumer Culture as a System of Wealth Production

Consumption refers to the 'social, cultural, and economic practices' related to the procurement, purchase, use, and disposal of valued goods (Bocock, 1993). It is a fact of life for all living things, and a function of all societies. Through definitions such as this, scholars of consumption remind us that these sorts of human behaviours are often achieved through non-market means and informal markets as well as through market means like shops. It is easy to forget this as a marketer, but it is crucial to consider potential competition from alternative channels such as auction sites. Otherwise, you may find your profit to be surprisingly absent one year!

As noted by Rassuli and Hollander (1986), **consumer culture** refers to societies where consumption is seen as a valid and central goal in life. It is theorised as distinct from **subsistence consumption**, in that it involves an increasing emphasis on consumption for expressive purposes. As noted by these authors, its emergence over time and space has tended to be accompanied by the development of **monetary systems**. One would think that money drives commerce simply because it makes it so much easier. It's also important to note that **wealth** in the form of piles of coins isn't very interesting or impressive. As soon as wealth creation began in earnest, people wanted to find ways to spend it that made it clear when out and about that they had money; and which showed others something about themselves. While the monetary system was only rudimentary in ancient Egypt (with barter persisting to a significant degree), the tombs of pharaohs reveal how much the society valued the display of personality and wealth.

These authors track how consumer culture also emerged in ancient Chinese, Assyrian, Greek, and Roman cultures. Can you spot anything in common between all of these societies? They were all at least somewhat imperial systems – whether this was done externally (via colonies or imperial control) or internally (where regions or groups within a society are stratified). Again, either internally or externally, these systems were produced by individuals who were willing to take power, and then use that power to create stratifications which furthered and legitimated their positions. This allowed them to have disproportionate access to consumption opportunities.

At the same time, this is not to say that every person who has more than average wealth consciously created the system of consumer culture. Loads of other people were always produced as consumers. As noted in the introduction, this served the dual function of creating wealth production opportunities for powerful individuals and motivating individuals to work. Based on this argument, you might wonder why it was employed in some places but not others – for example, why both free consumers and slave populations existed in Ancient Greece and Rome. There, we see that **slavery** is a product of war and distance – it is not something that we can really get away with doing to our neighbours on most occasions (Cope, 2015). History teaches us that there are some real bad apples in humanity, and given the chance they will provide nothing in exchange for the labour of others. Sounds extreme? In the UK we briefly had unpaid 'work experiences' for individuals attempting to leave the state welfare system.

Consumer cultures persisted throughout the ages, from the Ming Dynasty of China to the Tokugawa era in Japan, to Elizabethan England (Featherstone, 2007; Clunas, 2004). With the industrial revolution, we saw the emergence of true **mass markets** – those which sought to stimulate commerce by encouraging the conformist consumption of styled goods. Again, the overproduction of goods actually brought economic crises that tended to destabilise local economies both domestically and abroad, and as such people were quickly wise to the fact that its introduction was not always in their interests. In Mintz's case of the introduction of sugar (Mintz, 1985), while consumers were initially so excited for this convenience, they were later quite embittered (get it?!) by the unequal trades upon which their access to this commodity was predicated. As a refresher, this was often that they had to work long hours in terrible factories for deplorable pay to be able to buy this product...

Within consumer research, we often see a focus on **global consumer culture** – how the standards of (generally American) consumers and firms became mass marketed throughout the world with varying degrees of success. I argue that what is more helpful at this point is the notion of a **global system of consumption**. While dominated by the businesses of a handful of highly developed countries, what is really important is that it emerges for very specific reasons, and in an identifiable pattern. It is not just a spread of the **standard of living** enjoyed within these countries, but a stage in **development processes**. As we will see in the next chapter, it often involves the mass marketing of goods from the most developed countries, which legitimates the dominance of those countries in the eyes of individuals.

In the last 20 years, we have seen renewed evidence of the fact that consumer culture not only emerges for business, but also contracts based on its whims. Public commentator Naomi Klein noted this in her work on what she calls the **shock doctrine** – how powerful actors within business and government are willing to take any financial crisis and use it as an opportunity to grab a slightly larger piece of the pie. One of the first massive transformations of a developed economy can be seen in the case of Japan, where a string of economic crises began in 1990. This has continued into the crash of the Anglo-American and European markets in the wake of the Global Financial Crisis of 2008–2009. While this seemed like a shocking change in the funda-mental model of consumer culture, it was in reality the culmination of decades of contraction in **labour rights, real wages** and **value-for money** (Marazzi, 2011). All three of these are fundamental compo-nents of the sorts of 'trades' that are done within consumer culture.

We now see **consumer participation** (levels of spending) rising in parts of the developed world, such as the BRIC nations (Brazil, Russia, India, and China). On the one hand, this can be seen as an issue of **justice** (fairness), as these countries have long contributed to the global economy but have not benefitted from similar levels of **consumer enfranchisement** (opportunities to 'be made' as consumers). At the same time, we should be cautious of the fact that even the world's dominant economies do not guarantee their citizens consistent and growing enfranchisement – that instead, the model tends to exist where it's nec-essary to maintain **labour productivity**. The same disenfranchisement seen in more developed countries is not only possible but also probable within BRIC nations, as consumer culture is more of a 'phase' in devel-opment than a necessity. As noted by Lazzarato (2015, 2012), **indebtedness** can work just as well as consumption at ensuring that money is made, and people keep working. The notion that wealth will eventually trickle down and then stay is questionable, as it has not even persisted within the 'global centre'.

What it Means to 'Be a Consumer'

Here I seek to take this analysis further, considering what it must mean to 'be a consumer', if consumer cultures are systems of value produc-tion. This is an idea that was introduced and well discussed within our field by Firat and Dholakia (1998), who pondered why we would not rather think of our customers (and ourselves) as people. New work within our field has taken up this mantle, and it can be advanced even more by consulting the discussion above. Key here is the work of Giesler and Veresiu (2014). They argue that the idea that we are 'con-sumers' isn't just convenient business shorthand, but that the term refers to a politicised status which exists for functional reasons.

Prior accounts had established that being a consumer is frequently presented as a fun alternative to thinking of oneself as a worker or citizen, and this rhetorical transformation has generally facilitated the shrivelling of unions and political fora (Papacharissi, 2011; Cohen, 2003; Habermas, 1989 [1962]). Within contemporary neoliberalism, Giesler and Veresiu (2014) argue that this reaches new heights under contemporary neoliberalism, as getting to think of themselves as consumers is a crucial mechanism by which businesses and governments offload liabilities and responsibility from themselves, and put these upon individuals. The **duty to consume** whenever possible emerges as a responsibility within almost all contexts, in the 'post-political' world. This is often channelled into notions of **consumer citizenship**, where even goals which would have traditionally been covered by governmental actions (e.g. the funding of medical research) are increasingly expected to be legitimately funded by charitable and consumer expenditure (Cohen, 2003). They also find that even the poorest individuals in the world are being brought into this mentality, so that they will increasingly internalise the poverty and crises they face, and seek to resolve them by frugal and entrepreneurial means rather than state assistance. Where the term 'consumer' is used throughout this chapter, it is conversant with this analysis of its socio-historic meaning.

The model can be advanced further with one more component. Both globally and domestically, there are always categories of individuals who are effectively barred from obtaining legitimate status as consumers. Zygmunt Bauman (2013) provided the best account for this phenomenon, which he calls an underclass. The **underclass** is excluded from both adequate and legitimate work as well as consumption, creating the sense of a pointless existence. Bauman wants it to be clear that the underclass does not result from individual disinterest, but that it results from systemic socio-political forces (e.g. economic downturns, epidemic unemployment). The underclass does not emerge due to negligence, but instead is consciously created. The reason they are so valuable is that they can provide a moral compass point against which 'legitimate' individuals are meant to orient themselves. As put by the late comedian George Carlin, they serve to 'scare the shit' out of the middle class, ensuring that they keep going to work and not asking for too much. From a global perspective, these can be seen as existing not only within class-diverse societies, but also as part of the world system. Indeed, some countries may be seen as 'too far gone' or 'not yet ready' for the sort of **bottom-of-the-pyramid consumer socialisation** seen in Giesler and Veresiu (2014).

Elsewhere, it has been noted that consumer culture is increasingly the only option. The incursion of private interests into areas such as transit planning creates situations where individuals often have no choice about their ethical consumption – for example, they absolutely must drive a car to work. And as ownership of industry becomes increasingly concentrated, we rarely have the option to buy things from trusted or domestic firms. All of these are of course compounded by the fact that labour organising has been so disrupted under neoliberalism! Still, we are made to *feel* responsible, so we find ourselves struggling with the mind-boggling sense of feeling disempowered and empowered at once.

The situation was well summarised by marketing researcher Alan Bradshaw in his own approach to how we are made as consumers. There, he starts from Italian political philosopher Giorgio Agamben's work on **animality**. Agamben (2004) contends that contemporary society has stripped us of our humanity, and our capacity for political action. Building on this, Bradshaw (2013) argues that we are reduced to the level of animals, through the process of consumer culture. This is because the possibility and probability of political action is almost totally foreclosed for most people, which implies that they live a life without an ethical dimension (e.g. like animals, who don't make ethical decisions like whether or not to eat meat).

Ultimately, we see that the idea of 'being a consumer' is quite problematic. First, it is a very reductive and demeaning way of looking at people, who have needs and a life outside of market contexts – well, where this is still possible! At the same time, we see that 'being a consumer' is also a matter of privilege within both domestic and international economic hierarchies. We cannot ignore that it is a way in which many people would love to be debased! Oh yes, to have the problems of being expected to buy lots of things! A final, and related point is that this model is becoming less and less economically sustainable even within developed countries, where we see surprising crises in the provisioning of even basic goods and services. Indeed, the financial crises of the 21st century show us that development is not a one-way street, as the developed countries are seeing declining access to goods and services.

Reconsidering the Nature of International Marketing Relationships

Most guides on international marketing research and international consumer research argue that international marketing practice is quite hard, and that doing the work properly (read: without massive offence) requires careful coordination (de Mooij, 2019; Baack et al., 2018; Usunier and Lee, 2013; Czinkota et al., 2011). We are to engage in much the same research and segmentation practices as we do in our home countries. We are meant to know not only if individuals will buy products, but also why. We are to do **demographic research**, learning about their genders, social class (as locally defined), needs, wants, and desires. From there, complex portraits of potential **target markets** emerge. **Product research** should be done to understand if consumers use products differently in other countries. Multinational corporations should assess what parts of their offerings are desirable in comparison to local brands and **position** them accordingly. Firms are meant to adapt their products where it would make for a better experience, and ensure there is some genuine value created which merits inclusion beside existing offerings.

Some of the above texts would recommend fostering **brand communities** abroad just as one would domestically – referring to online or offline enthusiast groups related to your firm (see Schau et al., 2009 for a thorough review of the benefits). This is a highly advanced tactic, so it is perhaps unsurprising that this is the first place I ran into problems in conceiving of the international use of such practices. While I had originally thought that teaching this was essential for my strategy and consumer behaviour students alike, as the concept is so popular within the countries where I undertook my training (the United States and Canada), I found it to be a complete failure even in the relatively similar UK. As someone trained in the United States and Canada, where the concept of brand communities is incredibly popular, it seemed like heresy not to teach the subject to students. All said, I have given up after years in the UK as almost no students strongly identify with brands or product categories. Even subcultural affiliations appear rare in my classrooms. Among my students, who are perfectly well dressed and enthusiastic about consumer culture, the goal of acquiring ever-more and ever-more-expensive clothes in a broadly acceptable style seems sufficient – no need or great benefit from 'sticking out' and 'being unique'. Perhaps this concept is contaminated by American individualism…

This led me to think further about the limitations of applying standard practices abroad, and has in part inspired this entire text. In reading the histories we saw earlier, I saw more and more cases where international firms had imposed their goods, rather than seeking integration by the sort of kind, semi-consensual methods used within their home countries. By infiltrating a marketing channel (as we saw with Unilever in the previous chapter), consumers often have little choice but to buy a product from a multinational – even if a local alternative had at one point provided better and more desired value. It cannot be denied that a brute force approach has been central to the deployment of international marketing throughout history.

In identifying what the actual politics of this sort of marketing practice would be, it may be helpful to consider the concept of **relationship marketing**. While traditionally considered to be a strategy concept, it can be argued to be equally relevant from a perspective concerned with consumer welfare. The idea here is that marketing is all about building relationships between organisations and a variety of stakeholders. Relationship marketing stresses not only holistic thinking about marketing, but also thinking as if these were actual, interpersonal, one-on-one relationships. The idea is that most organisations would prefer to keep working with individuals they already have in their orbit, rather than try to influence new people every time. Even in cases where **repeat purchase** is not likely (as in funeral care purchase) or not frequent (as in car purchase), a customer is likely to talk to friends and family, so encouraging a positive relationship with them is thought to improve the success of a brand.

In understanding the implications of this tradition for international marketing, it may be helpful to think back to its origins. The tradition was greatly influenced by the social psychology literature on committed relationships such as marriage and long-term partnership. One commonly cited inspiration is Caryl Rusbult (e.g. as seen in Fournier, 1998; Ganesan, 1994), and specifically her work on **satisfaction**. Satisfaction in relationship psychology is seen as a consequence of **interdependence** – a state which exists when two parties want each other, but do not need each other. Interestingly, that describes **non-political situations** – those wherein neither party has a distinct advantage over the other. A consequence of this theory, which Rusbult found in practice, is that unbalanced relationships, where an individual has significant power over the other partner, can create an environment hospitable to abuse (Rusbult and Martz, 1995). From this sort of definition of 'relationships', one might have questions about whether marketing ones can ever be truly equitable.

Think back to Chapter 1. What sort of relationships have marketers historically had with their customers? What sort of power dynamics have defined them? Make a few comments in the space below:

....

....

....

....

....

....

....

....

....

....

....

....

....

....

....

Ultimately, I argue that the 'foundations' presented here provide ample evidence that marketing relationships have often been uncharitable... indeed, one could say that the 'abusive' relationship with consumers is fairly standard! While this may be a shocking contention to some consumer behaviour scholars, it is not necessarily so controversial from a strategy and practice point of view, where we've noted there is sometimes (though not always) an understanding of the real nature of the relationships afoot.

Questioning Diffusion Models, from Our New Global Foundations

Another area of consumer behaviour scholarship which can be newly-interrogated based on the foundations presented in this book would be the classic **diffusion of innovation model**. Pioneered by Everett Rogers (2003 [1962]), this model was first produced to explain how products move within a single domestic market. As seen in Figure 5.1, which was drawn based on ideas from Rogers' 1962 text, the model contends that only a small percentage of individuals are likely to jump at the opportunity to take on a new technology. After this, there is a small vanguard, then the diffusion through the majority of society (the middle of the bell curve), and all the way through to 'laggards' – the last to adopt.

Viewed from a world systems perspective, this model is highly problematic. The factors of education, aptitude, and interest which drive innovation can largely be seen as privileges available first to a small minority, as any product is distributed globally for the first time. Put differently, while many individuals in developing contexts are quite interested in, and knowledgeable of, new technological innovations, their access to these products may be limited primarily by their place within global systems of distribution (*and* labour valuation).

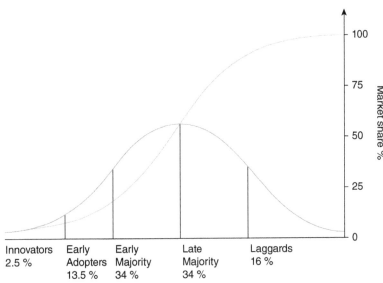

Figure 5.1 Diagram based on Rogers' diffusion of innovation (2003 [1962])

Unconvinced? Consider the case of Apple product launches, wherein the largest allotments of goods are designated for the United States, even where consumer demand and prices are higher in other contexts. By the sheer force of the firm's bias towards its own community of consumers and citizens, the diffusion of these innovations towards other areas is delayed. Perhaps we should not be surprised from a firm that often talks about its obscure hometown (Cupertino, California) in adverts, as if anyone outside of the United States could care.

Other examples can be seen in the diffusion of fashions. Big data sources, like Google Trends, show how fashions diffused not only over

Figure 5.2 An analysis I performed to show how skinny jeans usurped bootcut jeans. An unfortunate development for those who wanted to bend their knees everywhere. Author's own.

Figure 5.3 An analysis which showed the initial diffusion over space. Author's own.

time, but throughout the world (see Figures 5.2 and 5.3). Regarding the latter, it is interesting to see that the early spread of the skinny jeans trend seemed to occur mostly within English-language communities and through the Anglo-American region, but not within the European Union.

An important counterpoint can be seen in models of **meaning-making**, such as that of Grant McCracken (1986). This model differs from many in consumer research (and marketing!) in that it emphasises the disproportionate power of firms and powerful cultural intermediaries (such as television producers, magazine editors, and DJs) in shaping cultural tastes. Within global contexts, we see a hierarchical structuration of the field of cultural intermediaries, with those of the first world often being seen as more authoritative (Skov, 2014).

From 'Rational Choice' to 'Rationalising Choices'

Another set of models which can be reconsidered via the new foundations presented in this book are psychological models of **consumer decision-making**. These consider how people make **decisions** among the **choices** offered by firms. Important to note here is that firms do much to structure who gets what, when, and how in the ways in which they structure choices. Prices, as we have seen previously, may be set outside of an individual's reach, even if a much smaller amount is required for a profitable return.

Early models of decision-making assumed that individuals attempted to make rational decisions and that they had adequate access to information. In practice, this was seen to be far from realistic (Zey, 1998). In time, the notion of **bounded rationality** emerged, to factor in the limitations to an individual's options, as well as the relative value of rationality against other factors such as the speed of decision-making (see Solomon et al., 2013 for a beginner friendly review).

Critical studies from cultural studies approaches implore us to question whether firms really want us to make rational decisions at all. Charles Ackland (2012) and James Twitchell (1997) make innovative arguments here, in their work on **subliminal advertising** – adverts which are broadcast below the level of conscious perception (e.g. for so few frames of film that we do not notice the message). While the efficacy of subliminal advertising has never been demonstrated scientifically, each makes an argument about how our fascination with particularly deceptive adverts distracts us from the fact that marketers successfully deceive us all the time. Where we can see marketing materials, we are more likely to think they are fair, but in reality studies have shown that most of us are unable to process the always evolving array of tactics used to make our decisions imperfect.

Another marketing strategy which cultural studies scholars have argued triggers senseless consumption is that of **branding**. This term refers to the work of imparting a variety of meanings to goods to increase their value. It is argued that brands add too little value for the supposed status and affiliation benefits that come from their purchase (Twitchell, 1997). While this may seem like a quaint, old-fashioned activist argument in the neoliberal world of today, there is a simple economic logic under this: people could get significantly more real value from unbranded goods than branded ones, and they would enjoy what they purchase so much more. From a macro-level perspective, wasting money on such things is shown to make the world a more miserable place than it could otherwise be.

At the same time, we participate. **Materialism** – the unstoppable desire for goods and services – is argued to be an increasingly prominent social value (Richins, 2011, 1994), and this is seen as some sort of failing in our decision-making. **Personal consumer debt** like **credit card debt** has also been seen to be expanding without control in the developed countries of the world. Here, I question the notion that this is really 'irrational', or that simply becoming more aware of basic marketing tactics could solve the problem, as is often recommended by behavioural economists. Building on the socio-historic arguments at the beginning of this chapter, consumer culture can be viewed as a ubiquitous cultural system within developed countries. Once we leave formal education, we are exposed to few educational media. The media we *do* consume tend to be accompanied by commercial messages (by which I mean adverts!), and as we will see in Chapter 7 these are becoming more sophisticated all the time. Keeping abreast of every new marketing tactic would be a never-ending practice, and one that is likely impossible given that strategies are secret until they are used upon us. If anything, one could say that we are not trained to make rational decisions, but to *rationalise* our decisions. From fashion blogs to shopfront windows, marketing slogans implore us to view our purchases as somehow reasonable. Credit offers, which are available within our own online banking apps and at almost every till (in person *and* online), naturalise the idea that we can decide to purchase things we cannot afford.

These matters are only starker when we consider the global nature of the system of consumer culture. Given that firms are completely content to mislead consumers within their own countries, should we expect that they would act any differently abroad? No. Historically, we have seen that firms engaging in international operations have taken advantage of **information asymmetries** – the fact that they have greater knowledge about goods than their consumers – abroad in much the same way that they would at home. Given that the gaps in knowledge between firms and constituents are only greater in these contexts, we see that the degree of misdirection is only more severe.

For example, international marketing scholars have regularly critiqued branding for stoking the desire of products that cost far too much within local currencies (Baack et al., 2018; Usunier and Lee, 2013). As we saw in the last chapter, **deceptive pricing** is also a common misdeed, though one that is sometimes chastised. Within international contexts, firms have often been deceitful in describing what parts of a product or service were provided within a particular price. While mobile phone contracts in countries like the United Kingdom are regulated, and must say very specifically what must be included, in other parts of the world such regulations don't exist, and firms have been intentionally unclear about the charges that certain services would entail, and then have held consumers to these difficult-to-find rules. Finance charges for failure to repay, moreover, have tended to be ridiculously over-inflated. Across such gaps in language, knowledge, and culture, and given the blatantly deceptive intent of such efforts, why is it that we would expect anyone to act rationally (Zey, 1998)?

Case in Point

Development Discourse

In Chapter 3, we introduced critical discourse analysis as a method for questioning what is *really* meant within language. I find that it is particularly useful in attempting to understand many communications that are produced not only *to* consumers, but *about* consumers. Here I extend Giesler and Veresiu's (2014) examination of bottom-of-the-pyramid consumers by performing a critical discourse analysis of a statement by Melinda Gates (of the Bill and Melinda Gates Foundation). Here, I bring political economy into the analysis as well, considering how her statement is discredited by the financial foundation upon which she is making claims about Africa being backwards.

(Continued)

(Continued)

The video was created to honour Melinda Gates' work, but the statements by both the creators and Gates herself show a tremendous lack of understanding of how poverty was created, and the fact that mass consumer enfranchisement of the African subcontinent is unlikely under the terms set by firms such as the one she profited from. If that sounds like a stretch, just listen to the title... it's called 'Meet the Woman Who Wants to Save the World' (Now This!, 2017).

I have transcribed a few excerpts here, for your reference. The statements in quotation marks are from Melinda Gates herself, while the interleaved comments were text overlays from the video:

'We're trying to tell the world that progress is possible, that the world actually is getting better.' The Bill and Melinda Gates Foundation has invested billions of dollars empowering women and girls... Gates says the grassroots movements are being ignored and underfunded... 'We need to fund those women, because they know what is going on, that needs to be dealt with in their communities and they know how to get this grassroots change.'... Over the last two decades, the number of people living in poverty has been cut in half. 'But that progress is not inevitable. We have to keep up leadership, and we have to keep up funding... If we don't keep up this incredible generosity, this foreign aid the United States and other places give, this progress isn't going to keep happening. And we also have to be realistic about the fact that we're about to have the biggest cohorts of adolescents coming through the continent of Africa. And if we make the right investments for them, they will lift up their communities, and they will lift up that continent. But conversely, if we don't make those investments, it's a very different story. And so this is the time for us to have really bold leadership, and to make the right moves, if we're going to make the world better.'

At first glance, you may wonder why this is being cited as an example in a chapter on consumer behaviour. The point is that this text reveals much about people's myths about how the development of consumer culture occurs – both historically, and in the present.

Discourse analysis encourages careful investigation of words, phrases, and entire statements. Within this example, we can start with the use of the term 'progress'. What is Melinda Gates saying that progress is? She is referring to increased material standards of living, which given the poverty she is commenting upon, seems unproblematic at first glance. Discourse analysts tend to consider the wider meaning of terms from other studies, and here it must be noted that this is not likely an accidental choice of words, but part of a larger cultural myth – specifically, that of the progress narrative (Hickell, 2018). Progress narratives are argued to be highly influenced by a Eurocentric image of what development should look like, which has been occurring since early modern times. The adoption of this model has largely been in the interests of those powerful countries, and on their own terms. As noted in Chapter 1, we have also seen that countries *subject* to development programmes were originally not so far behind. This raises questions about Melinda's later comment that 'the world actually is getting better'. Here, we see a clear lack of understanding from Gates about how real inequalities in terms of wages and access to consumer goods evolved.

Later, we see the term 'empowerment', which in light of references such as Giesler and Veresiu (2014) becomes problematic. Here, those in developing countries are seen as incapable of producing progress on their own, and they are also seen to be in need of intervention from benevolent corporate overlord philanthropists. The cure to poverty is seen to be 'investment' and 'leadership' (again, from an American and European class of philanthropists and governments).

In short, the right to consume is something that is shown to be given as charity, despite the fact that integration into the world economy also serves the interests of the very corporations that made the philanthropists rich. This is where the real irony of such a statement can be seen. In the case of the Gates Foundation, their billions for charitable causes of course came from the fact that Bill Gates hoarded the economic returns from

(Continued)

(Continued)

Microsoft products. Rather than having spread them more consistently to workers and consumers over the years, he retained economic returns for his own purposes. Indeed, the Microsoft Corporation actually participated in economic policies which *held back* developing areas of the world, stymying consumer enfranchisement when it was not best for Microsoft's own wealth generation. In the case of China, for example, Microsoft was a part of the American Chamber of Commerce in Shanghai (Ruppel Shell, 2009), which along with the likes of Nike and Google worked to ensure that fair wages were not available for Chinese workers. While they claim that China has held back its own people, in reality they were personally involved in overturning one of the best-constructed initiatives to improve wages within the country. Now Bill and Melinda Gates are demanding wide-scale recognition for their great kindness, as they give some of it back.

Ultimately, development studies scholars have raised serious questions about the ethics of such models. While the texts are certainly worth a read, a lighter and more humorous introduction to the issue can be found in the Kenyan television show *The Samaritans*. It is a sitcom organised around a fictional charity called 'Aid for Aid', which appears to be interested in being seen to be contributing to poverty alleviation, but in reality turns out to be a highly fraught organisation run by misinformed white Europeans. Local employees are viewed as holding the real knowledge of the situation, and are portrayed as absent of naivety about the tenability of the organisation's mission. The 'boss' of the organisation, a posh white man of European descent, frequently refers to problems and challenges as 'African' – despite the existence of developed areas of the continent, and the fact that the continent is not an integrated political area in any sense of the term. Have I mentioned that the show introduces him as the Country Director/former intern (implying that he had leaped over local colleagues in his ascent)? In sum, this provides a *counternarrative* to dominant discourses of progress, market integration, and eventual consumer participation.

The Final Word: Ethics and the Global Division of Consumption

In concluding this chapter, I find it helpful to return to a concept from our foundation in ethics – the notion that there is a continuum from relativism to universalism. Kant famously called for universalist ethics, and philosophers such as Badiou are trying to bring this back in the contemporary moment.

What is the relevance of this intervention for the global stratification of consumer subjectivity, then? In short, it serves as a counterpoint to traditional, relativist notions about the ethics of this class-based division of the globe. Such a relativist approach would argue that standards of living legitimately vary based on culture – not as a result of historical or other formations. In turn, the differences in quality of living afforded to different groups are rationalised. The varying levels of material culture with which groups can support their traditions and rituals are naturalised.

What we see from a universalist perspective is simply that having values and traditions is what is common and defensible – not the notion that particular living standards come part and parcel with this. Moreover, firms should not treat individuals from different countries with different levels of respect. They should think of individuals across borders as they would their own. Common practices such as **extraterritorial** definitions of ethics (Baack et al., 2018) – those which accept different standards in different countries – are seen as questionable from this new ethical philosophy. An example of extraterritoriality in practice is the fact that we expect children in our own countries to play and even consume, while we accept (and some valorise) the fact that children in other countries are making the very clothes and toys our children consume.

While this new analytic approach may seem depressing at the outset, the point is again to reach a realistic understanding, which can be used to improve society for the better. Where consumer matters are concerned, a few important critiques emerge. To begin, we need to acknowledge that there are individuals who have decidedly bad ethics – who know that their actions are not benevolent and do not lead to net gains for humanity. The Gateses could be an example of this, as they cannot be blind to the fact that they have engaged in activism which literally restricted economic development internationally. While Melinda Gates may say otherwise publicly, it is unlikely that she is entirely blind to the hypocrisy of her own logic. Where firms do not realise that they have been subsumed within larger, regressive social projects, we should do what we can to expose this logic. At the same time, we must note the limited efficacy of such efforts, as the first class of actors are generally more powerful and do much to structure the world as they like it. Finally, and perhaps most importantly, we should do what we can to spread knowledge that one's success – or failure – to become a consumer subject is not actually a matter of individual effort. Instead, we need greater acknowledgement of how structural issues play the predominant role in ensuring who are the 'haves' and the 'have nots'. Within the context of the Global Financial Crisis, we also see a third category emerging – those of the 'have beens'. Further research into this area of experience within consumer culture will help us understand the entire lifecycle of being a consumer. Those of us who are enfranchised, and do have knowledge of this, should use the privilege we do have to push further in understanding and critiquing these matters.

Another potential approach has been identified within consumer behaviour by Ozanne et al. (2009). Rather than working from Badiou, they focus on the philosophy of Jürgen Habermas and specifically his work on the **public sphere** (1989 [1962]). This is an idealised concept from critical theory that concerns the terms where genuine communication could occur. In short, the ideal public sphere would be a place that is not dominated by the interests of powerful actors. Within political philosophy, the idea of **deliberative democracy** has experienced a bit of a renaissance, and it refers to spaces where people could deliberate upon ideas and develop socially valuable solutions to problems. Here, the authors expand on the deliberative democracy model and explain how the process could be used so that multiple stakeholders (government, citizens, activists, community members, etc.) could come together to make decisions on transport or global warming, given that it is unlikely that any one stakeholder can make the social change alone.

In closing this chapter, I ask you to perform a couple of further reflections:

What are your beliefs about how much you should consume? And how much your friends, colleagues and contemporaries should? How do you rationalise differences in entitlement and enfranchisement among your social circle?

....

....

....

....

....

....

....

....

....

....

....

....

....

....

How is your standard of consumer enfranchisement a product of the disenfranchisement of others? Consider, for example, what the cost of your mobile phone or computer would be if it were made by yourself or your neighbour.

....

....

....

....

....

....

....

....

....

....

....

....

....

6

Complication and Contention in Intercultural Interactions

Here, I will ask you to push your understanding of international marketing further. And what better way to begin such an investigation than... yet more questions!

Please take a moment to consider the following:

What sorts of international marketing topics and strategies interest you the most?

....

....

....

....

....

....

....

....

....

....

....

....

....

....

....

How many of these are *international?* In answering, try breaking down the word – international means 'between countries'!

....

....

....

....

....

....

....

....

....

....

....

....

How many of these are intercultural? In answering, try breaking down the word – intercultural means 'between cultural groups'!

....

....

....

....

....

....

....

....

....

....

....

....

Who do you think performs most of the 'international' work, within the organisation? And then, who do you think does most of the 'intercultural' work?

....
....
....
....
....
....
....
....
....
....
....
....
....
....
....
....
....
....
....

Based on my years of teaching international marketing. I find that the majority of students are interested in activities related to advertising, communications, and the like. International concerns – most of which can be subsumed within Chapter 4's models, such as PESTLE – tend to be less popular. Perhaps more importantly, they are often done by other divisions such as legal and accounting as much as they are done by marketing.

I don't take a stand on either being better or preferable. Where I do make a stand is that traditional international marketing strategy guides, like those I referenced and remixed in Chapter 4, often leave students and practitioners ill-prepared for much of what they actually want to do in international marketing. This chapter starts from the intercultural perspective mentioned in the Introduction, as I think it merits its own chapter just as much as traditional international marketing strategy and consumer behaviour. Here, we are graced to have a few excellent standards, which I introduce at the start. Still, this chapter is no different from the rest, in that I am not content to simply summarise the work of others. While intercultural marketing is already considered to be an advanced topic (though it shouldn't be), I want to push even this literature much further.

This is because I find that many major phenomena which emerge from scholarship on cultural politics – from battles for authenticity to cultural appropriation and cultural imperialism – have not been well integrated into international marketing thought, despite the fact that they intersect so much with actual international marketing practice. Here, I draw upon work from cultural studies, anthropology, and sociology. The majority of the chapter introduces these new conflicts and controversies, theorising them as part and parcel of the intercultural approach more generally. Building on this, the following principles can be derived from this chapter:

Principle 6a: As all modern nations are multicultural in some way or another, intercultural marketing principles have domestic as well as international applications.

Principle 6b: The 'international-ness' (or culturally defined character) of a product is often what makes it of value outside of its context of origin.

Principle 6c: The evolution of what is valuable culture over time can be best understood as a historical process – specifically, one where powerful cultures have imposed their standards upon others.

Introducing the Intercultural Perspective

Culture refers to the characteristics that define communities, making them distinct. In news reports and everyday conversations we often think of differences in **ideal culture** (ideas), such as **values** (things a culture holds dear), **norms** (rules), **language** and **myths** (stories).

Material culture is also an important part of the picture, and refers to everything from tools and clothing, to objects used for sacred rituals.

People often think that commerce is all about **material consumption** – selling *things*! At the same time, it must be noted that consumption is becoming increasingly immaterial as the economy becomes digitised – a matter I will deal with in more detail in the next chapter. **Immaterial consumption** refers to things like the consumption of services and live entertainment. An interesting example here is that of massage, spa, and sauna. Within some cultures (like in Japan and much of Northern, Central and Eastern Europe), these are beloved activities for individuals, groups, and families alike. Having many academic friends from these countries, I have learned to enjoy such activities and see them as a normal part of life. Upon moving to London, however, I found it very difficult to find a proper sauna, as the **cultural practice** of sauna attendance is much rarer in the UK.

Intercultural marketing refers to any marketing that occurs between cultures. It has emerged as a significant perspective within international marketing thought because researchers realised that many of the biggest and most interesting challenges of business practice occur because of *cultural* rather than *national* frictions. Mainstream treatments of international marketing rarely talk about the topic, and when they do, it is often in terms of linguistic faux pas – for example, not knowing that there would be an unexpected connotation of a particular brand name in a foreign country. While these are funny examples to read, they are really only the tip of the iceberg of intercultural marketing practice... and most firms now know to be very careful about who does the linguistic work, so these matters are no longer such a huge issue. More important considerations can be seen in the work of Marieke de Mooij (2019) and Usunier and Lee (2013), which I will discuss in turn.

De Mooij (2019) presents an approach that focuses predominantly on differences in cultural values, drawing heavily on a framework which comes from famous international business scholar Geert Hofstede. As noted by de Mooij, Hofstede performed a giant study of professionals across a wide range of cultural backgrounds, and argues that the following values can be used to explain how all cultures differ: masculinity and femininity; individualism vs. collectivism; fear of uncertainty; long-term or short-term orientation; indulgence vs. restraint; and power distance (tolerance of inequality) (see Hofstede, 1983, for original). De Mooij, meanwhile, charts how these may apply to every aspect of international marketing practice.

All said, there are some notable critiques of Hofstede's work. For example, many took offence when their country was defined as 'more feminine', and argued that perhaps they just had different notions of masculinity; the collectivist vs. individualist dimension, long-considered a hallmark difference between the East and the West has also been criticised as a changing phenomenon (de Mooij, 2019; Brewer and Chen, 2007; McSweeney, 2002; Schwartz, 1990). These models also risk reducing the diversity of human life to a handful of national cultures. In reality, identifications such as subculture may be more useful. **Subcultures** refer to groupings which have less authority than, say, Parliament, but which may nevertheless powerfully structure an individual's behaviour. As noted by anthropologist Dick Hebdige (1979), subcultural identifications are often communicated through consumer culture.

Usunier and Lee (2013) diverge from this fixed notion of culture, emphasising its complicated and localised nature. For example, they are quite interested in **cultural symbolism** – how different ideas are represented symbolically in various human cultures. They note that linguistic translation is rarely enough, as marketing communications such as adverts need to be **culturally translated** as well, to ensure that the symbols used within them are chosen to have the desired meanings across cultures! Branding, in particular, becomes complicated across cultural boundaries, given that brands are themselves constructed to represent a complex web of values. Elsewhere, the authors note how business practices involved in **business-to-business** (**B2B**) commerce as well as **personal selling** (or **direct-to-consumer** sales) may need to be conducted in different ways based on local norms.

Taken together, de Mooij provides a great introduction to why intercultural marketing is essential, as seen through an exploration of Hofstede's work. Usunier and Lee bring this down to a finer level, and allow for a wider range of definitions of culture. In both texts, the authors stress the importance of **market research methods**, which make it possible to understand – and ideally work cooperatively – with people from other cultures. Again, the rest of the chapter builds on their intercultural perspective, seeking to integrate some further intercultural issues from other disciplines within academia.

A key principle within intercultural texts is that organisations must constantly make decisions between **standardisation** and **adaptation**. Sometimes, these decisions are driven by convenience, as advertisements in one language can easily be run in another country that speaks the same language. Whether they can be *understood* equally well across cultures is a different matter. Canada, the United States, and the United Kingdom represent three of the remaining G7 countries, and their linguistic commonality and relatively high disposable incomes can make it a tempting proposition to attempt to advertise to all three. In practice, however, major differences in humour, slang, and symbolism can undermine such efforts, as well as the fact that each country has its own national economic and trade contexts. What may appear at first glance to be an efficiency, or a potential easy way to an economy of scale, may prove to be much more difficult in practice.

Ultimately, both de Mooij and Usunier and Lee find that adaptation is rarely as valuable as a company might hope, and instead think of the desire for standardised communications or offerings to be a distinctly American fantasy. In short, it is one that firms hoped was true, but which rarely is. It is in turn very dangerous for firms that aren't American, or aren't tremendously resourced, to engage in this sort of strategy. A classic example comes in discussions of the mass marketing of refrigerators within Japan (de Mooij, 2019). Japanese homes were much smaller than American ones, and Japanese consumers shopped for groceries more frequently than American ones, so large capacity units were unpopular. A more recent example is Starbucks who in their first attempt at entering the Australian market failed miserably due to Australia's thriving independent cafe culture, informed by a century of Italian and Greek immigration into Australia.

Another major question within this debate concerns **global branding**. While the notion of having a coherent, somewhat internationally consistent, worldwide business is attractive to many marketing novices, it is deceptively difficult to achieve. If you think about it, McDonald's 'I'm lovin' it' is not as much a standard to emulate, so much as being one of the rare catchphrases that could work in many cultures. Let's face it, it is a very generic sentiment. This explains not only why it works, but also why there can't be 15 McDonald's equivalents. There are not that many common sentiments, nor could loads of companies with very generic expressions be world leaders.

One important assumption which I always incorporate in my research and teaching, and which I would like you to take away here, is that there are often many different cultures within a country. Multicultural countries like Britain, for example, have significant variation in terms of language, cuisines, traditions, rituals, and preferences in material goods. At times, the notion of 'nation' may spread across territories, for example, Irish people live not only in the Republic of Ireland, but in Northern Ireland and the rest of Great Britain, as well as in the United States and throughout the world. French culture also spills across borders into neighbouring countries – not only Germany and Belgium, but also Britain, as London has been described as 'one of the largest French cities' by population numbers (Ash, 2012). In such cases, there may be important cultural trends that persist across such national boundaries. When this occurs for reasons of coerced immigration, this is often referred to as a *diaspora* – encapsulating the notion that a culture had been geographically fragmented unwillingly (Stacey, 2018).

There are also often cultural group differences, even within supposedly 'mono-cultural' nations. For example, there are very often *youth cultures* which diverge significantly from other groups. Gender can also be thought of as separating people into different cultures, though it is interesting that many work and live (though not necessarily socialise) across such lines. In short, the omnipresence of culture means that intercultural marketing has relevance whether or not one does international marketing practice in work (Principle 6a). Ultimately, adaptation and standardisation are matters to be considered across all sorts of cultural divides – not just national ones.

To truly understand the intercultural intervention, I recommend thinking through the following question:

What cultures would you find difficult to market to? Challenge yourself to think in terms of subcultures as well as national and ethnic cultures.

....

....

....

....

....

....

....

....

....

....

....

....

....

With these considerations in mind, we'll now try to think about even more complicated cultural issues.

Thinking Abstractly About Culture as Value

In the previous section on strategy, we discussed the importance of sustainable comparative advantage – something a firm holds over all others. Once one has determined what international opportunities are available, and which are advisable given the conditions surrounding the firm, the next step is to identify the smaller strategies of how this work is done. Often times, it is cultural meaning that is used to produce these sorts of competitive advantage (Principle 6b).

Indeed, the *international-ness* or *cultural character* of a product is a key driver of the internationalisation of business. Put simply, the buying and selling of goods and services is often predicated upon matters of cultural differences, exoticism, novelty, and culturally defined value (e.g. it comes from a high-value **culture of origin**). This section is organised around some key phenomena, related to the cultural nature of value in international marketing.

First, and most benign, is when a country or culture markets its own products based on their uniqueness or as mementos of encounters with the culture. Marieke de Mooij (2019) primarily talks about products with **culturally specific values** as something that we need to honour and make for particular segments, but this can also be a form of value ripe for commodification. Oh, goody!

One example of the cultural specificity of value can be seen in a case of limitations to mass marketing. American film and television has been mass marketed internationally, based on the sense that it would be universally desirable. De Mooij (2019) critiques this notion, saying that as countries have developed they actually tend to prefer local media content, in their own languages. Who would think? In any case, an interesting limit to the spread of American cultural products can be seen in television dramas sold within Latin America. There, adaptation to a *telenovela* format is often preferred. An example of this can be seen in the case of *Grey's Anatomy*, which had to be adapted by Colombian television makers to become *A Corazón Abierto* ('To the Open Heart'). As one can see from trailers and clips available online, this is a much more dramatised form of storytelling. It has its own conventions and plotlines as well. In time, Latin American cultural producers proved their value even further, as the *telenovela* format has now been marketed to a United States audience with *Jane the Virgin* (which was adapted from the Venezuelan *Juana la Virgen*).

Related to this would be issues of **tourism**. Here, local cultures are offered to visitors for consumer experience. At times, this can be quite well executed – particularly where locals are doing the work themselves, or where their input is involved. **Touristification**, however, occurs when the process is over-done, often by outsiders. One key case is that of the mass promotion of Venice as a tourist destination, which has impacted the ability of actual Venetians to enjoy their unique culture (Settis, 2016; Davis and Marvin, 2004). The city centre has no roads for automobiles, so one can only get around on foot or by boat, but tourists have clogged much of both.

At the same time, it has been noted that imagined disparities between ethnicities are often exaggerated within touristic promotions. In other words, local populations are often racialised, so as to emphasise what is supposed to be different between the consumers. Some particularly problematic examples can be found in the marketing of Australia abroad, as scholars have argued that indigenous people have often been needlessly portrayed as backward. They note that most indigenous cultures of the world are actually just as **hybridised** – mixed with other cultures and benefitting from intercultural developments in technology – as other cultures are.

Within the UK case, marketing researchers Burton and Klemm (2011) conducted an extensive analysis of travel adverts produced for UK travel agencies. There, they found that the vast majority of adverts studied featured only particularly light-skinned, white, presumably British tourists, and that locals were portrayed to be as dark as possible. These locals were often engaging in stereotypical behaviour. For example, Black male resort staff were shown as athletic performers in the majority of Caribbean holiday adverts, reinforcing stereotypes that Black men are strong but unskilled. This is unfair not only to those who are commodified, but also towards the customer base. The exact tourist agency office they studied was in a city with the UK's largest South Asian British population, and the authors argued that those individuals would also struggle to see themselves accurately portrayed. Taken together, these are considered to be problems in **cultural representation**.

Heritage sites like museums are often operating within these economies of culture, and engage in many of the same (often problematic) activities. To begin, the entire project of **museification** has been widely criticised, as its aim is the authoritative codification of cultures or styles, often without regard for the social groups from which artefacts originate (Iainniciello, 2018; Macdonald, 2013). Second, there are often questions of ownership, for example, the British Museum shows many works from Ancient Egypt and Greece that were the spoils of imperial domination, and as such not gained through legitimate, consensual means (see Figure 6.1). Meanwhile, the Greek people lose valuable opportunities to touristically present these materials within the area from which they came. At present, these are featured prominently within the British Museum's marketing materials – as the organisation sees their value for attracting customers as greater than the potential risk of angering or alienating those from cultures which might have a better claim to these cultural products.

Figure 6.1 The 'British' Museum has been widely criticised for its collection of antiquities from countries which might benefit from the tourism that would come with displaying them in their countries of origin. Photo by Furante (CC BY-ND 2.0).

Similar questions of ownership arise in debates about appropriation. **Cultural appropriation** refers to the use and often sale of culture by those from outside of it. The original cultural meanings are often lost, derided, or trivialised in the process. While this may sound like a grave statement, consider a classic form of cultural appropriation: the adoption of Native American adornments as Halloween costumes by white, likely European-descended people in the United States. Elsewhere, in cases such as the popularisation of 'world music' within the United States, there are questions of **exoticisation** – using the culture of others simply as something different and novel, with little interest in the actual cultural reasons why it is different. Musician David Byrne of Talking Heads fame critiqued this industry roundly (Byrne, 1999), finding that it reflects a false interest in diversity among record labels and consumers alike.

Appropriation is a complicated matter, which has led to a great deal of confusion, as the creative use and remixing of cultures has occurred for centuries. The point at which it often becomes controversial is when the original **creative labour** is uncompensated, and the rewards are large. A major legal case concerning this dilemma emerged in recent years as Urban Outfitters was shown to be mass marketing Ethiopian and Eritrean cultural garments without any understanding of their original meaning, and without compensating the identifiable artistic community wherein the designs had originated.

When those in the *developing* world engage in intellectual property theft, it is often judged much more harshly. For example, there are several websites which mock the use of broken English in tattoos and apparel from abroad – as if mis-appropriating foreign languages is not something that English-speaking designers and consumers also do! And while fashion designers regularly take from those in developing countries without compensation, the same courtesy is rarely shown to people in developing countries who copy designer styles. This is often subjected to harsh counterfeiting litigation, resulting in exorbitant fines that those in developing countries will struggle to pay.

Cultural Imperialism: The Imposition of Cultural Values from the Centre, Internationally

Take a moment to consider the following.

What cultures do you look to for value? How do you think they gained that position?

....

....

....

....

....

....

....

....

....

....

....

....

....

....

The final principle of this chapter (6c) concerns how 'what is valuable' is negotiated as a socio-historic process, over time. Here, powerful countries have often asserted their own values upon others. As noted in Chapter 1, European colonialism was a pivotal moment in the expansion of this sort of commerce. One horrifying example can be found in Anne McClintock's work on how British soap brands were marketed aggressively within the African colonies. One advert for Pears' soap, for example, depicts a crowd of dark skinned 'tribesmen' who are shocked to find a message on a rock saying that 'Pears Soap Is the Best', accompanied with a tagline that says Pears is 'The Formula of British Conquest' (McClintock, 1994: 225). Numerous other adverts imply that dark skin is a sign of being dirty, including a subset which imply that perhaps blackness could be washed off entirely with soap (see Figure 6.2).

There were of course cleaning practices in place within these countries, many of which better served local needs, but the strong, normative messages in these adverts convinced many that they must consume in order to fit in.

In time, it is said that a sophisticated system of cultural imperialism has emerged. The previous versions of imperialism focus predominantly on economic and military tactics by which force is gained over the territories and livelihoods of others. **Cultural imperialism** refers to the export of ideas from the centre to the periphery, which ultimately has the effect of making individuals more sympathetic to imperialist nations, and their cultures more similar. It is often accompanied with aggressive marketing, which makes the continued persistence of local culture difficult. Because of this, Edward Said (1994: xiii) referred to cultural imperialism as 'The power to narrate, or to block other narratives from forming and emerging'.

Classic cases have focused on how media productions such as television and literature have been mass marketed not only for profit, but also to contribute to the project of world economy formation. Said, in the work above, looked particularly at novels such as the work of Rudyard Kipling. At the same time, cultural products for children were

Figure 6.2 Advert for Pear's soap, which visually equates blackness with dirtness. Public domain (published 1884).

seen as a particularly valuable site of intervention, given that their attitudes about culture and international relations would not be particularly well formed. Ariel Dorfman is a noted scholar here, as he identified narratives which lionise imperialism in studies of Donald Duck (Dorfman and Mattleart, 2019 [1971]), the Lone Ranger, and Babar (Dorfman, 2009).

A more recent example, which I explore with students in seminars, concerns how private healthcare in the United States is perceived by those outside of the country. Among those I teach, the sense is that the standard of healthcare people receive in the United States is excellent, and that facilities are almost exclusively the most sophisticated. People believe that Americans almost always have private rooms in hospitals. In time, this may be softening attitudes towards the privatisation of healthcare in other contexts like the UK. In reality, as an experienced user of American healthcare and well-read person on the subject, I can say definitively that private healthcare does not always mean better. Within the United States, it is simply the only funding model, and there are certainly terribly funded private facilities. Indeed, research shows that providing services with as much administrative bloat as the American system has simply doubled the cost of health care, compared to the United Kingdom (*BBC News*, 2018b).

It is also important to note that ideas are communicated not only through cultural products like novels and films, but also through advertisements and consumer goods themselves. For example, the export of the mini-skirt carried with it ideas about gender and sexuality that were unremarkable in the United States, but highly objectionable in some receiving countries. It is argued that consumer culture as a whole ultimately becomes a standard towards which people feel compelled to conform. Üstüner and Holt (2010) considered this in their study of the domination of (a particularly American incarnation of) consumer culture within Turkey.

Cultural imperialism is not something that must happen across national boundaries either. As with Usunier and Lee's argument that we should think *interculturally*, rather than internationally, we can see how cultural imperialism may occur very frequently within multicultural societies. The rise of far-right movements across Europe shows how particular dominant groups within these countries tend to have a single, culturally specific idea of the nation (and its consumer traditions), which is then imposed upon others.

Often times, such divisions are defined in terms of race. Cope (2015) notes that there is no inherent set of 'races' within humanity, and that any such claims are better understood in terms of **racialisation** – the identification of often arbitrary visual differences in bodies as a justification for the creation of race-based class differences. From cases like those from McClintock (1994; discussed above), we see that cultural imperialism often occurs across racial lines – as they exist both between and within countries.

Within European and Anglo-American societies, it is argued that an aesthetic of **whiteness** permeates the highest echelon of cultural productions. This has led to the mass marketing of products which impose white beauty standards onto other bodies. Within the United States, the emphasis on 'whiter' hairstyles is pervasive in the Black community, a phenomenon which Chris Rock critically (and playfully) discussed in his documentary *Good Hair* (2009). There, he claims that his daughter at the age of four had told him that she was told her hair was 'bad' for not having been subjected to massive amounts of processing already. This emphasis on conformity to white culture permeates not only hair-care products, but also fashion. Given the dominance of European and American cultures within the world stage, Cope argues that whiteness becomes a standard internationally as well – an example of which can be seen in trends towards epithelial fold (eyelid) plastic surgery within East Asian cultures.

When revealed for what it is, however, cultural imperialism has been judged harshly. In many cases it has been taken as a target for activists. Key examples can be found in the fights against cola giants like Coca-Cola and Pepsi. A particularly humorous example comes from Turkey, where a nationalised cola was important to the domestic economy. They hired Chevy Chase for a series of advertisements which mocked Coca-Cola's and Pepsi's efforts, quipping instead that perhaps the United States would be unable to resist Cola Turka. In another advert, the company shows an American army member crawling across the desert to find a cold Cola Turka – a prospect which leads them to much delight. Historically, the American military had brought consumer products (more commonly chocolate) into conflict contexts, which was seen as one of the 'delights' for exhausted combatants and civilians alike; here, this narrative is reversed to comic effect.

Elif Izberk-Bilgin (2012) has looked at such contestations in Turkey more recently, examining how it has transformed with the growth of Islamic culture. She finds that certain brands – interestingly, including Coca-Cola – are seen as *haram* (forbidden), not because they contain cultural content that is specifically anti-Muslim, but as Coca-Cola has been a commercial bully within many Arab countries. Nokia, meanwhile, is seen as a positive example, as they developed a phone that included prayer time notifications. This was seen as a very positive way of working with a culture different from one's own (Nokia was based in Finland at the time).

Finally, it should be noted that incursions can be in terms of **retailing**, as well as through media and communications. Using marketing channels, marketers have often found it easy to impose products upon other populations. Unilever is a classic example, as they have largely worked to get a small set of brands established to serve certain functions (e.g. shampoo, soap) throughout the world. While their offerings are unlikely to have the same history and cultural meaning as local ones (for example, they do not adapt their scents to local cultures), they have managed to succeed nevertheless by simply outdoing their competitors on price margins. By becoming the shopkeeper's favourite, they've become the global leader – without even becoming the consumers' favourite (Hoogvelt, 2001; Perlmutter, 1969).

Questions of Authenticity in a World of Hybridity

A major controversy within cultural negotiations is that of what counts as **authentic** (see Gilmore and Pine, 2007 for more information). This is particularly heated within international marketing, as that which is deemed 'more authentic' is deemed worthy of greater cash value. At the same time, such negotiations are not so simple; sometimes customer bases are more interested in what they perceive as authentic (Beverland and Farelly, 2009). Many curries popular in the UK, for example, were in fact produced here specifically for British tastes.

A great example for exploring this and other questions can be found in Jeffrey Pilcher's (2012) work on the marketing of tacos (and Mexican food more generally) outside of Mexico. Pilcher finds that a handful of American companies are largely responsible for mass marketing this food internationally, as Mexican firms have historically struggled to have equivalent capital and resources to do so. At the same time, this has meant that the Mexican people have lost control over popular understandings of what tacos are. Pilcher notes that in Norway, for example, tacos are often considered to be an option one might have on an 'American food' night, much like hamburgers. Hey, it's all as American as pepperoni pizza... which is itself Italian. Wait, is it possible that cultures are rarely as separable as we might think?

What Pilcher finds in the Mexican case is quite shocking! The country had petitioned to the United Nations to have their culinary traditions protected as an official matter of cultural heritage. The French jury rejected the initial petition, however, based on grounds that it was not of an adequately peasant origin. In their apparently professional opinion, authentic Mexican food was not what Mexican people would have considered it to be!

Pilcher also highlights a surprising paradox. Within the United States, he sees a rising popularity of Mexican food, but also persistent issues of racism against Mexican Americans. He addresses this issue most deeply in a dedicated chapter concerning how taco trucks that serve Latino communities are often seen as a nuisance and subject to complaints and fines, while many of those complaining likely enjoy Mexican food in other contexts. I find these matters have become pronounced with the election of Donald Trump, who had previously referred to Mexicans as rapists and drug dealers. At the same time, many of his high-profile officials continued to eat at Mexican restaurants. The Internet was in turn filled with stories about how Mexican restaurants had rejected these individuals and other Republicans (including everyday voters), but the early stories turned out to be rumours.

In time, however, this idea of not serving conservatives has come to fruition. While there have been several occasions where Republicans have recently been refused service (one high-profile one was that Sarah Sanders had been ejected from a restaurant for her anti-transgender politics), there was one incident which finally, perfectly summed up the politics of liking Mexican food, but not Mexican people. Homeland Security Secretary Kirstjen Nielsen had been delighting in consuming Mexican food, all the while executing Trump's plan to keep (predominantly Latin American) refugee children in concentration camps – a move that was swiftly met with criticism (Rosner, 2018). At this point in history, one can only wonder – are we seeing Pilcher's critique gain traction? Are the seemingly impenetrable cultural contradictions of loving a culture's food, but hating its people, being rightly criticised as unjustly racist? Only time will tell how these cultural politics eventually play out.

Case in Point

Cultural Issues in Scandinavian Design

One context I often use to explore cultural issues in international marketing is that of 'Scandi design'. While Scandinavian design traditions are of course as heterogeneous as any other culture's,

(Continued)

(Continued)

internationally the term generally refers to mass-marketed functionalist designs. It's interesting because they were initially very culturally-specific but are now ubiquitous throughout the world's urban areas.

Functionalism is a design philosophy which stresses that the function of an object is meant to predominate its design, rather than purely visual aesthetics. Functionalist design was a counterpoint to various forms of ornate, but less useful, design which were popular in Europe for centuries. Importantly, they were not necessarily meant to be more expensive, either; the goal was to provide a good quality, long-lasting product within a price range that consumers could afford. Bright colours were often used, inspired by the notion that everyday items should be stimulating and enjoyable (see Figure 6.3 for an example of a flat designed in such a style; for further introductory discussion see Ashby, 2016; Wilhide, 2016; Fiell and Fiell, 2013).

Figure 6.3   Apartment with Scandinavian style furniture. Photo by La Belle Gallerie (CC0 License).

In time, original Scandinavian products have benefitted from positive **country of origin effects**; in other words, there is quite a premium which comes with products that are seen to have a more 'genuine' and 'authentic' connection to this tradition. At the same time, the meaning of the style began to drift, with the country of origin effect sometimes predominating. Teak furniture, which was produced most widely by Danish designers, became incredibly popular even though it was often not very functional. It is a rare wood, which at the time could be pricey. This encouraged the use of cheap veneers which were easily damaged. Where full-thickness wood was used, many purchasers did not know how to treat it properly for durability. Sounds more like 'dysfunctionalism' to me!

In time, the functional school has been mass marketed internationally. While this originally started with the export of goods produced within these specific countries of origin, foreign designers eventually learned how to imitate and even copy the styles. While functionalist design enthusiasts would know the real thing from the imitation, many other potential customers would be unable to tell such differences, or even care that they were not authentic. For those interested in falling within a particular **aesthetic** (visual design) trend, rather than embracing the full value of functionalism (e.g. through durability), cheap 'knock-offs' can even present an opportunity. British brand Habitat is famous for such designs (though has struggled in recent years), and other key makers of Scandi furniture outside of Scandinavia include another British brand, Made, and the French brand, Maisons du Monde. Within architecture and interior design the most easily imitated elements (like bright colours and simple, blocked designs) have diffused so widely throughout the global economy that their origins would be unintelligible to many. Examples of this can be shown in Figures 6.4 and 6.5, which show the deployment of these styles within London. This spread of aesthetics-sans-value can be seen as either a tremendous victory or terrible defeat of functionalism on the world stage.

McDonald's has started using various types of Scandi designs within their restaurants (see Figure 6.6). These redesigns have come alongside new initiatives for higher welfare food, better sustainability and improved nutritional content. Depending on your evaluation of their evidence on these points, you could either see this as a valid pairing of design and dining,

(Continued)

(Continued)

Figures 6.4a and 6.4b   Examples of the thousands of deployments of mass Scandi/fast Scandi in London. Author's own.

or a case of 'Swede-washing' – where the firm is trying to create a responsible impression by invoking popular conceptions of these social democracies. One matter is much more certain – they have in fact violated generally agreed-upon rules for the reuse of design styles. They produced chairs that were so similar to those from the studio which produces Arne Jacobsen designs that the restaurant chain was accused of 'pirating' a chair (Isherwood and Litterick, 2007).

Figure 6.5 Scandi redesign of UK McDonald's restaurants. Note the chairs which are inspired by functionalism, but ultimately not very functional as they are neither comfortable, durable nor easy to clean.

(Continued)

(Continued)

At the same time, firms from Scandinavian countries have also been known to modify their design values for mass markets. Swedish IKEA is the largest and best known for the sale of this style not only internationally, but also within the furniture market in general. Whether the design is truly 'functionalist' is a matter of debate, however. There have been many critiques of the firm's penchant for practically disposable design quality, which would arguably undermine all claims to serious functionalist design. IKEA defends this practice, however, by saying that their production methods are developed to optimise the use of the world's timber – of which they are the largest purchaser. By producing products at low prices they are also striving to disseminate simple, useful, and reasonably sustainable furniture to the largest market possible.

Figure 6.6   How IKEA bookshelves are used in real life, outside of Sweden. Photo by Yellow Dog (CC BY-SA 2.0).

Here, we must ask ourselves another question: is it so simple to spread culture? Does it just need to be shipped across the world on a container ship, assembled by hand, and voila! – respect for functionalism has also been exported? The wide availability of 'IKEA Fail' pictures on the web would indicate otherwise, as the ethos of decluttered space (as seen in Figure 6.3) is of course not universal. An example of this can be seen in Figure 6.7 below, a typical example of what IKEA Billy book-cases look like outside of their native habitat in Sweden.

Of course, one could also question whether this design madness is an ideology within Scandinavian countries as well, which would lead to judgement of those who do not appreciate it. There are also questions about the respect proffered to particular designers and the various countries. The term 'Scandinavia' (and the 'Scandi' that is now commonly used) is problematic itself, as many feel that it downplays the diversity and differences within the countries. Finland, for example, has a very different language and a complicated political history with Sweden. Norwegian design often differs greatly from that of Sweden, Denmark, and Finland, while Estonian designers wish that more would consider Estonia a part of Scandinavian modern design. While some view it as the sort of monolithic thinking that tends to come from the outside, we see a case of self-commodification in a highly controversial campaign by Stockholm's city branding professionals. Researchers have critiqued how Stockholm declared itself 'the capital of Scandinavia' – a move in which Sweden reinforced this notion of a 'cohesive' region and managed to anger the rest of the (at least imagined) region by declaring themselves de facto leaders (Gromark, 2017; Dobers and Hallin, 2009).

There are also questions about whether functionalism has just become a sort of new 'design imperialism', as it has so much value internationally and yet is only one of the many styles that humans could use to decorate their surroundings (Brunnström, 2018; Murphy, 2015). While originally intended to bring good and plenty to many, some have argued that it is an example of how the visual culture of the Global North is seen as valuable and even superior, despite the fact that there is no objective criterion upon which such an evaluation could be made (Escobar, 2018).

The Final Word: Thinking Critically about the Cultural Politics of International Marketing

Taken together, matters of culture in international marketing can seem overwhelming. That said, there are a few basic considerations which can help make sense of the territory. First, you may simply ask yourself what your relationship is to any culture you may be promoting. Is it your own, and are you presenting it as universal? In cases where you are promoting something from your own culture, is this tacitly valorising norms from your own culture – for example, does it promote whiteness as somehow virtuous and universally desirable?

Alternatively, are you profiting from another's culture? If you are, then how can you ensure that you are not doing something offensive? Here, it is important to note that not all use of other cultures is appropriation. Enjoying a meal at an ethnic restaurant, run by people of that ethnicity, is not appropriation – though claiming it as 'your food' would be. Here, you should ask yourself: can you compensate those who have contributed to the production of the value? Are you affecting the authenticity, and if so, can you reverse your direction? Can you refer to the product as something like 'Tex-Mex' food, rather than Mexican food? Producing questions like these in response to the ideas in this chapter will help ensure that you market culture in a way that is locally sensitive, and fair to those who have produced the value.

As with many of the other phenomena investigated in this text, negotiating these matters can be done carefully and ethically or through brute force. Where marketers have huge power advantages they have often been insensitive, as they do not need to do otherwise to be successful. This may even be a situation in which you find yourself, in business practice. There, it will be up to you to decide whether to take a more ethical direction. In making choices, you should consider not only ethical principles, but also what is learned from the historical and political perspectives. As seen in these chapters, social conditions change, and being the successful but arrogant company may ultimately be a poor long-term option.

PART III

Envisioning Futures

While Part II sought to bring existing international marketing scholarship into conversation with our new foundations, Part III goes even further, taking this conceptual exercise into the *future*! Well, as much as we can… There is ample evidence to support the notion that new media technologies and sustainability will be two of the biggest challenges facing international marketing in the future, so I have taken those on as the contexts for this section.

My initial, gut-level impulse has always been to see these two as opposed. The scientific community has of course raised serious concerns about the sustainability of even our high-tech present… much less the mass diffusion of these technologies that many envision for coming years. Here, we must acknowledge that not only climate change but also literal resource availability will be major problems *within our lifetimes*. All of this is on top of issues of **economic sustainability** – whether the uneven, exploitative division of labour will be tolerated in the future. Most of our beloved electronic devices are produced under some of the world's worst labour conditions, and yet they still cost a fortune. If we reach a point where individuals refuse to work under such conditions, our seemingly endless stream of smartphones, tablets, laptops, and who-knows-what-is-to-come, will find its end.

At the same time, many believe that scientific developments will bring us a technological fix for all of our problems. This includes not only environmental ones, but social ones. Among technology professionals and academics alike, the notion that despotism and other evils could be circumvented by new media technologies has been popular for quite some time. Some even believe new communications technologies and the digitisation of consumption could reduce the carbon intensity of our lifestyles such that we could avoid the climate apocalypse. This includes international marketing efforts, where there is a hope that many of the traditional challenges of internationalisation could be erased by technological developments in logistics and communications.

This is not an unchallenged opinion, within academia or elsewhere. In the era of fake news and misinformation, popular mistrust of new media is perhaps reaching a new high, as many wonder whether they had been fed false promises. Moreover, we see that we have not entered a carbon neutral age, but in fact the most carbon intensive period of human history.

Ultimately, this section seeks to reach a realistic, evidence-based approach to evaluating the relative benefits and disadvantages of technology on a burning planet. Chapter 7 on new media disabuses readers of the notion that new media will change everything, thus making the work of international marketing a doddle. It then considers the strange visions of technology mogul Elon Musk as a window into what is to come – or what should be stopped at all costs! Chapter 8 brings an up-to-date scientific perspective on the state of the environment into international marketing practice. Here, we question the underlying notion of internationalisation, which is generally a more carbon intensive form of commerce. Think about it… why *is* it that it makes sense for the modern, developed countries of the world to ship products to and from each other, when in reality many could produce (or at least source) whatever they like much more locally? The most recent International Panel on Climate Change report is the 'futuristic' vision in the final section, as it provides insight into the truly hellish existence which is expected to be realised sooner rather than later. It is important to note at this point that this is already a reality for many in the globe, who live in parts of the world that are already tremendously affected. At the same time, we can see some insight into what would *have* to change elsewhere. The chapter concludes with a consideration of my own work in the Toronto local food scene. This again takes a Badiouian perspective, revealing the true causes of climate change inaction.

Ultimately, many of our 'utopic' visions have problematic elements in terms of scientific feasibility, economic sustainability, or likelihood of democratic access. At the same time, they nevertheless remind us to remain open to possibility, and to think critically about whether there are in fact new technologies that could improve the lot of humanity. They also encourage us not to be complacent, thinking we have some-how made it to the technologically informed future. It is possible that the best (or worst) may be yet to come.

After Part III, the book reaches a brief conclusion, which will urge readers to integrate the concerns of this and all other sections into their future international marketing practice.

7

New Media Utopia?

New media refer to any communications medium which has emerged in the last 20 to 30 years. One of the most striking things about new media are that people tend to have very extreme opinions about the subject. Many business students and practitioners are effusive about how they think it will 'change everything'. The enthusiasm is only greater when discussing new media in the context of international marketing, as there is often hope that new technology will be a long-awaited remedy for persistent problems of cultural and physical distance. At the same time, there are those who worry about its difficulty, the cost of transitions, and even the potential for new forms of surveillance.

As with many other topics in this book, this is an area where our initial impressions may mislead us – and unfortunately, there is little practical guidance to be found within traditional international marketing texts. Most comprehensive international marketing textbooks spend *very little* time on new media... in spite of great interest in the subject, *and* the fact that new media are not even that new anymore! Where new media are mentioned, it tends to be a one- or two-page extension of an existing communications chapter. Marketing communications texts frequently do better to keep the pulse of technological developments – but there, the international component is often given short shrift! Both of these add-on approaches do little to advance knowledge of this subject. And of course, both of these are 'trickle down' disciplines.

Inspired by these elisions, the main goal of this chapter is not only to perform a fusion of these two literatures, but also to advance it with recourse to proper 'parent' disciplines. This is yet another site where our 'foundations' (in history, ethics, and politics) can help us produce a better understanding. Luckily, however, we do not have to go back quite as far as we did in Part II, because critical media scholars have already done much to 'digest' the implications of those traditions for new media practices. **Critical media studies** helps us to think clearly about the real characteristics, benefits, and limitations of new technologies, rather than acting upon unfounded hopes and fears. I introduce the approach in the first section, and then present a handful of key findings from past international marketing communications research which fit well within it. This leads us to the two principles of the chapter:

Principle 7a: In identifying the role of new media in international marketing practice, it is essential to separate our beliefs from reality.

Principle 7b: While new media have special benefits (e.g. decreasing the cost and timeline of international communications), many of the same principles of marketing and communications apply to these media as well.

As this is a chapter within the 'future' oriented part of the book, however, we will not just stop by applying critical media studies to marketing theory. We will consider whether there are any new theories of international marketing communications to be derived from this tradition. With this, later parts of the chapter consider new and pressing issues in the deployment of new media globally. Particularly provocative is a close-up on the beliefs about technology and development held by Elon Musk – a leading designer of electric engines, solar panels, artificial intelligence (AI) technology, and space exploration devices. Here, we see both the value and dangers of what some call 'technology ideologies' – beliefs about progress and development which diverge greatly from reality. On the one hand, these visions can inspire the development of technologies that improve human life; but we also see cause for concern, especially concerning their uneven accessibility throughout the world.

Before we start this work it's important to take a moment to reflect upon what you think about new media. That way, you will be aware of how this may be influencing your practice, and what sections may be of greatest relevance. To that end:

How do you communicate, receive entertainment, and find information? Consider the full range of options you use. For 'extra credit', you may want to take some notes on your personal use of these media, over the next few days – something anthropologists refer to as **fieldnote taking**.

....

....

....

....

....

....

....

....

....

....

....

....

....

For each, what are your beliefs about their popularity? How many others do you believe use the same platforms? Where would they be located? Are there barriers to their use of these technologies? If so, what sorts?

....

....

....

....

....

....

....

....

....

....

....

....

....

....

As mentioned previously, taking a moment to reflect like this is called **bracketing** within the social sciences. The practice emerged in the second half of the 20th century, in response to critiques about whether social science can ever be truly 'unbiased'. While it is not expected that one can completely eliminate their biases, it is important to understand how they may affect one's reasoning. From there, critical thinking encourages us to challenge those biases, and even look for *counter-evidence* which may dispute them. In our most advanced forms of social theorising, exploring our bracketed assumptions can even help us develop theory, as we work to understand our relationship to the world around us in abstract terms.

Introducing Critical Media Studies: An Approach for Thinking Deeply About New Media Practices

Christian Fuchs (2017), a leading proponent of critical media studies, argues that many people tend to make decisions about media practices based on **technology ideologies** – beliefs that we follow as if they are truth, even though they are not. Ideologies are produced because they tend to serve the interests of those who produce them; as such, we are most likely to adopt the ones that already fit our beliefs. Fuchs finds technology ideologies to be highly polarised, and he explains that this is because they are based on desires or concerns. **Cyber utopians** focus on the former, and believe that technology is inherently good. Some, for example, think it will bring peace, prosperity, and democracy to the masses. **Cyber dystopians** focus on the latter, , worrying that new technology will only worsen social problems (e.g. allowing those who are already powerful to expand their **surveillance** capabilities).

One would think that the solution must be that 'neither ideology is right, the answer is the average of the two'. This is not *exactly* the case. Fuchs' finds that technologies are often neutral in the abstract… but that they can have either positive or negative effects once embedded within social life. Moreover, any single technology likely has varying effects across demographic groups, as the world is a stratified place. What is good for the wealthy in one country may not be helping those struggling in another. With this in mind, Fuchs provides some guidance for thinking more critically about media:

1. In investigating some *particular* media practice, we should begin with a neutral position (bracketing assumptions, as we did above!).
2. Then, we should remain open to the full range of possible effects media can have. Even in the abstract, they may have specific characteristics – for example, high-tech development is more 'material' and polluting than we often think. Once embedded in the social world, again, the potential for misuse only grows.

3. Based on a **political economy of communications** perspective, Fuchs argues that we should take into account how media practices are made meaningful by the larger surrounding political economy. In doing so, we should look out for both local and global influences. For example, it should be of interest to those *outside* of the US that two companies based in that country own the majority of the world's social media space (and with it, revenue).
4. Given the ascendance of neoliberalism globally, this tends to mean that communicating is a political game, and one which favours the powerful.
5. Evaluating whether that is 'good' or 'bad' depends on the ethical framework you are employing. If you are operating from some sort of capitalist economic philosophy that believes the powerful should be entitled to any value they can harness, this would be good! If you come from a more critical, liberatory ethic that would be interested in equality of access to media, this is not so good.
6. Often, the final answer is that any particular medium has 'mixed results', though biased towards the most powerful. For example, a social media platform may be pivotal in a particular protest, but it is more often used by advertisers and promoters.

Where new media are used by marketers, we should expect it to be no different than any other practice – in other words, it is often politically deployed. Again, this is because organisations are competing with each other, and are in an inherently adversarial relationship with customers, in the pursuit of maximal value.

A few further concepts are also helpful, in understanding the implications of this perspective for international marketing communications. The first is that of **affordances**. Originally termed by Donald Norman (1988), the term refers to anything that a technology can do for an individual. While this concept may seem too obvious to even mention, it leads us to a couple of important considerations within a critical perspective. It reminds us that the benefits of technology can be *very* medium specific, so that we do not assume that what works on one platform will work on another – even two seemingly similar ones like the aforementioned Twitter and Facebook.

There are a few key affordances where new media are concerned. To begin, it is undeniable that web-mediated technology has made international communications cheaper and faster. What once took weeks via mail or post, or which cost a fortune by landline telephone, can now be accomplished by more efficient means. So **speed** and **cost savings** are sometimes (but not always) affordances of digital technologies. **Anonymity** is an affordance which can be quite unique to new media technologies. This has benefits to businesses at some times, but can also be a liability, as customers block organisations from accessing their data. **Interactivity** is an aspect of daily life, as well as social media, but obviously social media provide opportunities for interacting with a greater number of one's contacts in a given day than would be possible through traditional means. Ultimately, it must be acknowledged that many new media have more affordances in common with an older technology than with each other – for example, television and YouTube are similar in that they both transmit video, and some visual conventions work better in video than others.

Another key concern of Fuchs and many others within critical media studies is questions of **media ownership**. Here, a critical perspective urges us to be attentive to the **concentration of ownership.** While ownership may be concentrated anywhere in an economy, it is particularly pronounced in contemporary **mediascapes** (the media environment available to an individual or organisation). With the growth of multinational corporations, we see unprecedented conglomerations of media enterprises, such that a very small number of corporations control a huge portion of the world's **media diets** (content consumed). Australian-born Rupert Murdoch has been a widely critiqued owner of media within not only Australia but also the United States and the United Kingdom. Many have been concerned that newspapers such as *The Sun* and *The Times* in the UK, and television outlets like Fox News and Sky, serve to legitimate the concentration of wealth and power in the hands of a few. Elsewhere, social media 'sharing' tends to mask or redefine corporate communications as personal ones from friends. This is done because we do not like to be fools, and are mindful of where messages come from, attempting to **decode** them – but here and everywhere, marketers are always working to stay a step ahead.

The dominance of corporate communications from a handful of owners also causes tremendous problems for businesses that seek to advertise. While marketing communications texts often wax poetic about the beautiful limitless 'space' on social media, it must be noted that *valuable* webspace is much less common. While it may be cheaper than some traditional spaces (like the New York print edition of *The New York Times*), the costs do add up. In turn, the notion that '**barriers to entry** are minimal online' is both true and untrue. Yes, it is undeniable that content *can* be put online cheaply, but placing it where it will be noticed by a great number of people is another matter entirely.

Taking on these concepts, as well as the critical perspective, the next section identifies some of the best work that has already been performed within international marketing and marketing communications. Later sections will push this further, drawing on advanced topics which have not been covered at all, or in such detail. Considered in light of the above approach, the problem with past international marketing thought on new media becomes apparent. Much of the past literature has tried to skirt around or downplay the political nature of marketing communications. Here I argue that this is a disservice to all – whether you have the most conservative or liberatory views – as it does not provide the most accurate understanding of the subject.

Rehabilitating Past Work on New Media in International Marketing

International marketing scholarship on new media which adopts even an iota of this perspective tends to come from one of two sorts of author: those who do advanced intercultural marketing research, and those who do advanced marketing communications research. Sadly, there are few authors who really excel at both, simultaneously! I identify a couple of key interventions very briefly here, but as with the other chapters of the book, do not see this as a fulsome introduction to any of them. You may want to follow up with the texts cited to learn more details about each. Again, this chapter seeks to bring together the best of what exists and push it significantly farther… and into the future!

First, as noted in major social media marketing texts (Dahl, 2018; Fill and Turnbull, 2016), old media still exist! Indeed, they are often used in *conjunction* with new media, rather than simply disappearing. E-retailers, in particular, often need to use traditional advertising to get potential customers to the site. This is particularly important for international marketers to consider, as e-retailing is often considered to be a quick and easy way to overcome the massive barriers that existed when retail occurred exclusively via actual shops. One would be surprised how much of the same set-up is required to gain traction in a new country! New opportunities also mean more noise, as all other businesses have these channels at their disposal too!

Cultural issues of *understanding* persist, and a great deal of cultural work is often required for international marketing to progress productively (Usunier and Lee, 2013). In particular, **cultural translation** is required, just as much as **linguistic translation** (de Mooij, 2019; Jandt, 2013). De Mooij reminds us that this applies not only to advertising, but also to the marketing of media and communications – like music, books, and literature. Consumers are becoming more resistant to cultural imperialism and are rejecting both standardised and culturally specific (but not local) content. For those who have been raised within a dominant economy, this may be surprising, but try imagining the converse. If you are not Korean, how much of a K-pop song would you understand? At the same time, De Mooij does not see this as a simple 'success' story, with cultural imperialism all but gone and markets 'giving people what they want'. She notes that the ownership of media is often contracting, which means that imperialism is just evolving to be less perceptible. Sounds problematic!

The next sections will now present a variety of advanced concepts in new media practice for international marketing, informed by critical media studies concepts. In some cases, these will be matters which have been largely missed in past texts. Others are much-needed extensions and updates.

Questions About the Availability and Popularity of New Media Technologies

The actual popularity of new media in particular cultural contexts may also be over-estimated or biased by the popularity from one's own country. International marketers frequently believe that whatever platform is most useful and accessed within their own country will not only exist elsewhere, but will also be used the same way. It is often the case that *neither* of these assumptions is true. Some particularly miserable faux pas can be seen in European and Anglo-American companies' assumptions about what social media are popular in China. Here, issues of not only *culturally specific preferences* but also *barriers to access* have been ignored, as organisations have failed to stay abreast of what has been censored or is currently considered to be needlessly risky to visit.

I discovered a fascinating example in an unexpected place, in the course of a specific research project. I was performing a major study of the Occupy Wall Street encampment in New York City, with a special interest in the movement's media practices as news sources were *abuzz* about their revolutionary potential. I engaged in participant observation at the protest camp site (i.e. I lived there!), and found that those in the camp rarely used social media as their phones were always dead. Later I interviewed one of the movement's main Twitter account handlers, and I found that their communications were often a one-woman job!

After the encampment disbanded, I decided to study the news reporting critically. I was shocked by what *The New York Times* had been reporting, as they declared that many movements were Twitter revolutions when later research has largely disproven this. They had even re-used the idea of 'the first Twitter revolution' several times, as uprisings grew in size from Moldova to Yemen, Libya, Tunisia, and Iran. By the time of the Tahrir Square revolt (Cairo), one would think they would have learned, but they had not. They reported that Twitter was absolutely instrumental, when in reality one of the most pivotal days occurred when the government had shut the platform down – which ironically motivated people to go into the streets to see what was happening (Fuchs, 2017). Even so, the adoption rate of Twitter in Cairo was only 1 per cent at that point! Eventually, they had to issue an apology for their overzealous, non-factual approach to the role of the media in these movements. Unfortunately, it was already too late – that article never received nearly as many views or shares as the original, click-bait worthy ones!

Let this be a cautionary tale for all ye international marketers, and would-be ones. Even highly trained, reasonably critical journalists at *The New York Times* got completely swept up in social media fever, and specifically in the idea that platforms popular in their own countries were used widely. Even worse, it was often lazy journalism, based on screen-captured Tweets in English… often indicating that the social media posts were by outward-looking (and frequently elite) users. Especially in the early days of these revolts, the *convenience* of new media appeared as a siren's song, and sadly replaced traditional on-the-ground journalism. For this reason, a sophisticated and critical approach to media recommends combining methods which capture personal accounts of historical events and media practices, as well as study of the actual new media content itself (e.g. Tweets) (Fuchs, 2017; Costanza-Chock, 2012).

As with consumer culture, we must also consider the **global dispersion of technology**, and how that has historically come to pass. There are of course tremendous disparities in access to new media, largely shaped by the imperialist and now also neoliberal global political economy within which we are embedded. At the same time, we must note that as communities develop, they do not necessarily follow the original linear trajectory taken by more developed countries. An inspiring example can be found in the rollout of 'mHealth' apps and telephone services in many developing countries (reviewed by Gurman et al., 2012; Krishna et al., 2009). While in-office appointments seem a standard approach to medical condition maintenance within highly developed countries, and phone-based services may seem strangely futuristic, they are simply practical and elegant solutions where basics like transportation links are lacking.

Another set of excellent examples can be found in work on **frugal innovation**, where those in developing countries seek to find more economically (though not always environmentally) sustainable approaches to locally producing technologies similar to those in more developed countries. Electricity production tends to be a key focus here, which has ultimately yielded advancements in technologies such as solar, which then find applications within more developed countries!

Issues of Persuasion in International Marketing Channels

Marketing communications texts give some consideration to the notion that new media are not excellent substitutes for traditional marketing strategies. For example, e-retailing and chat services tend to be a poor substitute for traditional retail, in product categories where purchases are high risk (e.g. expensive, difficult to assess from a distance) (Fill and Turnbull, 2016). This is because face-to-face communications are highly adaptable and are some of the most persuasive in a wide range of social contexts – not even just in marketing (Cialdini, 2009). While valuable in and of itself, this is an analysis that would benefit from expansion with critical media studies. Moreover, there are specific considerations that come from international and intercultural contexts which have not been well integrated, so there should be interest in internationalising this discussion.

Couple this with the fact that international marketers are gagging at the opportunity to web-mediate their practices, and you have a perfect storm of poor performance. You can Tweet to people in Sri Lanka all you like, but if they cannot find you, and if Tweets aren't as interpersonal as other approaches, this may not be very effective at all! This would especially be the case if the Tweet was not done in the local language. If you are doing these things, maybe you should fire your social media manager...

These issues can be somewhat ameliorated where firms work to inspire interactive social media behaviour around your brand – e.g. by **seeding** potential content to popular social media users (often called **influencers**), in the hope that they may begin the viral spread of a video, or they may endorse a product by taking a 'selfie' with it. This is because **social media word-of-mouth** is highly persuasive as it 'feels' like it comes from friends – who we naturally trust more than any marketer. This is a reason for international marketers to be genuinely enthusiastic about new media, as social media can at times achieve even greater results than traditional tactics. Of course, one has to do the legwork to get individuals to that point, and that often involves the traditional tactics and old media communications anyway... but still. We can cautiously say there is potential for legitimately new communications opportunities where social media are concerned.

At the same time, we should note that persuasion can also be affected by the damning imperialist histories we have recounted in the chapters which have come before. One country with a significant history of anti-imperialist consumer protest is that of India, beginning with Gandhi's hunger strike against the commodification of sea salt to more recent boycotts of Monsanto 'suicide seeds', which die after a single harvest. While Monsanto ultimately prevailed in that case, it was nevertheless a battle.

Surveillance, Predictive Analytics and the Death of Privacy

One narrative which does have some particular value is that 'new media affords marketers new surveillance opportunities'. Traditionally, gaining information on whether consumers actually saw ads, and actually made purchases, was almost impossible. As the famous quote by John Wanamaker goes, 'Half the money I spend on advertising is wasted; the trouble is I don't know which half'. While this sounds like a joke, it was a problem that plagued advertising since its inception. Within marketing scholarship, econometricians spent decades of their lives trying to model whether a particular television advertisement might actually lead to increased sales. Given the tremendous expenditure involved in purchasing that sort of advertising time, the audience interested in the answer was quite great.

This is of course a question to which answers will never be objectively known. All of that changed with the advent of new media, as it finally became possible to track responses. An early and still ubiquitous form of marketing surveillance can be found in the case of **cookies** – data beacons which websites leave on one's computer. Email versions of direct marketing appeared quite early as well, and involve links that can record which particular registered user was taking advantage of a particular promotion. **In-app purchasing** provides similar opportunities within games and utilities on a range of devices.

A particularly innovative strategy in recent years is called **profile porting,** which is where one uses their social media account to log in to other services. With services such as Spotify, porting was originally introduced as a way to receive the service for 'free'. Critical media studies scholars would be quick to note here that commercial providers rarely provide anything for free – for example Dallas Smythe (1977) was famous for his analysis of the **audience commodity**, or the way in which we exchange viewing ads (like on TV) for content. We continue to do this on platforms like YouTube, and this reaches a new height with porting. There, customers are exchanging data for access to content, and this can become more valuable than we imagine. In time, profile porting has become so ubiquitous that we hardly notice it anymore, and we increasingly see it as a convenience – for example, it is not uncommon to 'port' onto Spotify *as well as* paying for the premium service!

This is a development which is concerning even in domestic contexts, and those who study it in international and intercultural exchanges find that it can be significantly worse. Kira Strandby (forthcoming), for example, found that mobile phone data rates in Ghana are punitively expensive – often many, many multiples more than customers within the United Kingdom pay for the same bandwidth. This is already terrible practice, as international marketers should set prices at a sensible rate for local communities. Even more disturbing is that the system exists to encourage mass porting of information. This is because Facebook has collaborated with mobile data providers to offer any content on their site at hugely reduced rates – leading to a state where many individuals have to go through Facebook to get all of their information about family, friends, local events, basic information *and* news. For many adopting web-mediated technology for the first time, data-tracking will be a part of their experience from the beginning onwards. Imagine if everything you ever looked up on the Internet since the age of 12 was logged, tracked and analysed for maximum profitability! Actually, that's increasingly not too difficult to envision... what a terrifying prospect!

Here we must also note that the transition between accessing web-based content at home, versus via phone, is not one that has simply 'emerged naturally'. It is one that powerful actors have largely encouraged and orchestrated. This is because data porting is made so much more valuable when one attaches smartphone location **metadata** to it – information about all of an individual's movements in physical space as well! It is more and more common for apps to request location permissions, and even so, it only takes a few tracking-heavy apps (like Facebook) having this permission to generate an unbelievable trail of data behind an individual.

Initially there was hope that this could at least be subverted in international contexts. How would it be possible to make sense of an individual's movements, in a country that speaks a very different language? Ha! Tricked you, capitalism! Unfortunately this state of affairs did not last long at all. Have you ever used Google Maps? What about when you have travelled abroad? Seems handy, doesn't it? Google seems to know what businesses and government agencies and whatnot are *everywhere*. I hate to disabuse you of any illusions, but mapping technology isn't just some benevolent project. They have translations of those maps into any language they like. In turn, they can track how often a woman of a certain age calls her mother, and then goes to her doctor, and then goes to a drugstore, and then... what we have is a pregnancy algorithm. **Algorithms** refer to identified patterns which can have predictive value. Originally hatched within countries like the United States – retailer Target, for example, found out that when women in their thirties bought cocoa butter for the first time ever, they tended to be pregnant (Duhigg, 2012) – they then send heavy marketing communications and promotions to these individuals, often using address information associated with their debit and credit card accounts. In time, it proves to be an incredibly effective strategy, as people tend to consume the most when they are in life transitions. 'Catching' those individuals is the game, and now with metadata, this model can be replicated in every country in the world without knowing a single word of local languages.

In time, this becomes a business model in and of itself, as Google sells access to this data; sells analyses of the data (**data-mining**); and also provides organisations with opportunities for **targeted advertising** to these individuals. Indeed, they cooperate with credit card companies, social media firms, and app developers to facilitate this process – leading to the critique that it is really *big collusion* and not big data which is problematic (Turow, 2017; Robson and Olavarria, 2016). This leads to the shocking era of **predictive analytics**, wherein tremendous data *about you personally* can be used to guess what you are likely to buy next and advertise that to you relentlessly. The case of pregnant women is a par-ticularly interesting example, as it leads us into one final direction... that of children. As young people all over the world access these tech-nologies at younger and younger ages – indeed, they are often the only accessible routes to certain types of information, as in the case of mobiles in Ghana – their **preferences** can be shaped before they even exist independently. In time, this has led to concerns about not only **privacy** (the right to be unknown), but also **social engineering** – that firms can create us however they like. In time, we see the increasingly sweeping, undemocratic ordering of our lives – which we nevertheless feel as our own (Sunstein, 2018).

Of course, the previous chapters in Part I and Part II show that mar-keters have been shaping our subjectivity for centuries... we just previously had a sense of control, which some scholars say can be even more dangerous (Ackland, 2012; Twitchell, 1997). It is also true that they may be getting much better at it, which should raise concern. Indeed, it's so concerning that Trump personally believes digital media aren't worth trusting, and he sends anything he wouldn't want subpoenaed via registered human couriers whose jobs depend on not leaking information (Colvin, 2017). This is perhaps one of the only arenas within which Trump has a good idea.

My goodness. It's a scary new media world, isn't it? While it may seem exciting as a marketer, we need to keep in mind that we are all consumers too. This means we should have an interest in *resistance* to these new initiatives. Let's go *there* in the next section!

Consumer Counterattacks: How Surveillance is Undermined

These new opportunities may require **consent** in new ways, too. For example, consumers need to opt in to text messaging services or download an app and accept notifications. Compared to direct mail, where businesses can simply buy a list of addresses, often sorted in terms of interest and demographics, gaining access to people's most valued media outlets can often be a challenge.

This can also be a case where the 'national' meanings of international marketing can rear their heads. The recent roll-out of new privacy protections in the European Union, for example, have caused a huge panic among organisations throughout the world, as they had to quickly reconfigure their communications processes to meet this legislation's requirements. Many consumers were previously completely unaware of cookies, but recent changes to EU data protection laws have changed that. This may be increasing awareness of online monitoring that is taking place. That said, critics also say that the onslaught of GDPR cookie messages, which do not have to be standardised across sites, confuse customers and they may actually opt in more than before.

Privacy advocates have viewed this debacle as a moment to try to gain new adherents to the cause of **anonymous browsing technologies** including tracking-free browsers and VPNs, but many of these technologies are cumbersome to use at present. For example, many users find the experience of a tracking-free Internet to be surprisingly inconvenient, as they must always enter passwords and services like e-retailing may not work well with certain privacy systems in place.

Filtering technologies also prove to be a difficult wall to traverse for many marketers, as consumers may simply block their advertisements, or have them relegated to a dark email purgatory that is rarely if ever opened. Firms are clever here too, however. For example, as I sat down to write this chapter, I noticed that promotional emails ended up within my Google inbox, for no explicable reason. Google has the right to do this occasionally, when it thinks that they are important messages I might want to see. Sure, Google. It's no coincidence that it is in the prime e-retailing season before Christmas… This is a case where issues of **ownership** become prominent once again, as those that own the filtering technologies can also choose when they should be breached – and often gain a percentage of the profits where sales result.

The difficulty of ensuring that one is in contact with the most appropriate advertising vendors escalates exponentially when one works internationally. While it is often thought that content can be placed on the web and it will be found by interested constituents, this is not the case in practice. International marketers must dedicate personnel and finance to not only securing appropriate advertising space, but also engaging in **search-engine optimisation** (**SEO**) – ensuring that one's product appears as high in search results as possible in a variety of markets, and with the right sorts of search terms and cultural associations (de Mooij, 2019).

New Media, New Management: Labour Conditions on the Internet

It is also notable that new media affordances are also changing the labour market for marketing and related business activities. Originally, many championed the Internet, arguing that it would create new employment opportunities as industrial and manufacturing sectors sagged in much of the developed world. Generally, this has not been the case. It has been found that technology has generally displaced a greater number of jobs than it has created (e.g. through the mechanisation of production, or the use of automated sales staff) (Rossiter, 2016; Scholz, 2013). Some foresaw this, and hoped that the efficiencies would be distributed fairly, such that we could work less and have more leisure time. Employers have, of course, taken advantage of these developments to hire less staff. Those who remain are expected to work at higher and higher levels of efficiency, and marketing labour is a key site of change (Delfanti and Arvidsson, 2019).

A key site of changing labour practices in new media can be seen in online personal sales. Even in conservative industries such as banking, personal sales through **chat technology** is increasingly common. Between the fact that textual technologies do not require exquisite spoken language skills, and the fact that the labour market has become increasingly globalised, this work is increasingly outsourced. Platforms such as this often assign workers work names which are typical in the culture in which one is working (e.g. 'John' and 'David' when dealing with British customers). **Content moderation** is another rapidly growing field, as many labour to ensure that the content we see regularly is no more disturbing than it already is. Commentators have also raised concerns about the working conditions of those who do this work as they generally labour far from the home countries of their firms, for poor pay, with intense hours and duties, and with little public knowledge of their plight (Roberts, 2017; Cherry, 2016; Dyer-Witherford, 2015). In these ways, the digitally mediated world in which we live is not only dependent on unsustainable material technology (think of all those servers!), but also on unsustainable, unjust labour relations.

Here we also see an interesting twist to the Marks & Spencer case. The firm which has historically prided itself on supporting British employment and production came under intense scrutiny as it recently outsourced its IT operations to India (BBC, 2018a; Griffiths, 2018). While this is a very common practice, it is worth considering specifically in terms of the history we have discussed in Part I. The deployment of information technology jobs by American, British, and Canadian organisations is only possible as a result of the history of British imperialism within the Indian subcontinent, which has led to an uneven division of wages. A second legacy of colonialism is that English language skills are unusually common in India, compared to other developing contexts. Without this foundation, high-tech outsourcing would not be possible.

M&S made some statements reminiscent of their past outsourcing efforts, indicating that they had no choice but to make efficiencies, but they were not so strident in communicating that they generally had an anti-outsourcing ethic. Interpreting these statements in terms of the history of the company, many have argued that earlier outsourcing (of manufacturing) paved the way for this later outsourcing – and even worse, that the new outsourcing was not really necessary.

In other words, while M&S may have initially hoped to maintain their anti-outsourcing ethics, the very practice of outsourcing may slowly erode one's position. In time, one's original values risk being forgotten. While the Badiouian perspective on ethics discussed at times throughout this book encourages thinking of one's options as being more socially determined than we like to think, it also urges us to make commitments and 'not forget'. There is a warning that engaging in a compromised activity, even if it is the best available, could lead to eventual co-optation. While M&S seemed initially aware of this and wanted to resist, we see an eventual collapse of position.

Case in Point

The Cyber-Utopianism of Elon Musk

As promised, I believe the case of Elon Musk's cyber-utopianism is a fruitful context for exploring these competing theories and ideas about new media technologies. To facilitate that, I will begin with a very brief introduction to his major business practices, derived from his major biographies (McKenzie, 2018; Vance, 2016), before turning to analysis based on the theories from this chapter.

An interesting point of entry to this discussion comes by way of considering what *other* biographies Amazon suggested to me as I sought to learn about Musk. Based on sales trends, Amazon also suggests we read about Steve Jobs (Apple founder), Phil Knight (Nike founder), and Jeff Bezos (Amazon founder). The only identifiable commonality between these four individuals is that they became super-wealthy and influential US-based CEOs. For example, while three are dedicated to technology, this does not apply to Nike. It is notable that Amazon thinks of Musk first and foremost as an American-based CEO of large corporations, who has benefitted from tremendous amounts of start-up capital, and then also as a 'technology maven'. The underlying economic and political foundations of not only Musk's firm, but American neoliberal capitalism more generally, will become relevant as we proceed.

Elon Musk grew up in South Africa as a socially ostracised nerd (no judgement! I'm one too...). From his youth and into the present, he has been highly influenced by science fiction, and particularly the work of Isaac Asimov. He learned to program at an early age and a game he produced at age 12 can still be found online. In the late 1990s, Musk set up an online financial services company, which would later become a part of PayPal. He received a significant payout for that, and is generally credited as a founder of the organisation given the importance of his component – even though he was technically never an employee of PayPal. He decided to use the funds from this to start a variety of companies, all of which are focused on developing super high-tech solutions to the

(Continued)

(Continued)

problem of climate change. Keep in mind, this was the era of Al Gore's *An Inconvenient Truth* (2006) – a moment where climate change and sustainability were frequent news items, and when it seemed possible that major change could happen (e.g. if Gore had accepted his electoral victory – remember, Bush did lose in 2000!).

Musk joined Tesla and soon became its primary designer and eventually CEO. There, he set himself to work on an ambitious goal: the production of electric cars which were not just functional, but *sporty*. Rather than slowly, incrementally improve public perceptions of such cars, he sought to symbolically destroy all notions that they could not be high-performance. This idea in itself is very representative of his overall vision – which seeks to preserve all of the excesses of capitalist consumer culture, but without the environmental burden. His interest in electric sources of energy quickly spread into a related enterprise that produces solar panels.

Figure 7.1   Elon Musk and The Mars Society

His overall vision of humanity (including where it is going, and what should be done about it) is by far the most shocking. Musk's worldview is shaped by the notion that the planet itself is too unstable as a foundation for human life. He views Mars colonisation as a necessity not only due to global warming (which he'd gladly see prevented), but as any number of natural disasters could cause a mass extinction. With this in mind, he launched SpaceX, where he does not settle for the simple task of solving shortfalls in the US space program… by himself. No, he also is working on increasingly-reusable and sustainable interplanetary transport. He is proactively preparing to put a human on Mars in the early 2020s, aiming for having a Mars colony of 80,000 by 2040 (see Figure 7.1 from an address he gave to The Mars Society – an organisation that is dedicated to this goal).

Because of this, many of his terrestrial technology programmes are guided not only by their Earth uses, but also their potential towards this utopic goal, which seems swiped straight out of one of the sci-fi novels he would have read growing up. This includes not only electric cars and solar energy generation but now ultra-high speed, ultra-low energy travel via underground tunnels. Plans are already in the works for a tunnel between Los Angeles and San Francisco that will allow travel at over 700 mph, and Musk has his eyes set on the Northeastern corridor (from Washington DC through to Philadelphia, New York, and Boston) as the next goal.

At first glance, Musk's plans seem… absurd, and even impossible. It must be acknowledged, however, that he has already done many things that were not expected. He does engineer electric sports cars; he has developed the newest generation of space rockets; and Musk is making excellent progress in producing increasingly recyclable space travel units. There is even a test track of the ultra-fast tunnel and car system. His and others' visions of an electric energy future may be one of the only plausible ways to save humanity from climate change without requiring such radical cultural change that no one will do it – a matter we will discuss in more depth in Chapter 8.

All of this raises important ethical and sociological questions, however. To begin: is human life truly so intelligent and worthwhile that it merits saving, at all costs? Would an extinction that

(Continued)

(Continued)

harms humans – but not *every* other life-form – be so bad, or would there be an opportunity for something better to evolve? And most importantly: who would it be that would be allowed to join the colony?

At the end of the day, it is this last question that reveals the most about Musk's fantasies: 80,000 is *quite* a small number compared to the entire human population, so any Mars civilisation would automatically be an elite one. As life would be very challenging on Mars, and would presumably bias selection towards highly educated individuals... like Musk himself (discussed in a somewhat more balanced light by Davenport, 2018). So what else is entailed in the notion of 'a society of Musks', besides the fact that they'd likely be technologically adept? As Musk is fairly vague about who he would like to send to Mars (saying little more than the fact that he believes there is a need for artists as well as engineers), we must turn to his much more specific statements about ideal life on Earth for insight.

To begin, he is a fanatic about the United States as a social and economic project, from his youth when he dreamed of joining the techno-elite in the global centre. He describes his economic politics as 'fiscally conservative' and thinks that an independent, free market system is virtuous. He is critical of the notion of subsidies, despite having received many. For example, despite the fact that he no longer needs money, he took a $750 million subsidy from the state of New York in order to build a solar plant which would create jobs – though many believe the plant has not been fully developed and is underperforming (Rodriguez and Groom, 2018). He has been criticised for not even allowing the most minimal form of wealth-sharing for his Tesla employees: unionisation. His policy on the matter is well explained by Lopatto (2018), who sees this as part of the wider culture of Silicon Valley tech capitalism. Recently, Musk has even been accused of 'rage firing' plant workers (Duhigg, 2018).

None of this bodes well for a potential worker's utopia on Musk's Mars™. With Musk at the helm and little in the way of taxation or regulation to stop him (and even subsidies to help), he can arrange much of the US high-tech sector around his plans for a Mars colony.

In the event that he does colonise Mars, such a privatisation of power means that we would likely have little say in how it was governed or structured. Perhaps the term 'colony' is surprisingly apt for what may come, as the settlement would be a very self-interested plan, and one which might become very indifferent to other forms of life (e.g. on Earth). This is a far cry from the actual visions of Musk's hero, Isaac Asimov, whose fiction was concerned with the abuses that can come from capitalism, colonialism, elitism, and social exclusion (Asimov, 1980).

While this may all seem completely remote to our subject of discussion – new media and international marketing! – it is telling of the overall political economy within which we operate. Here, theory on the political economy of ownership can help us understand the potential pitfalls of not only Musk's enterprises, but others. Musk's various undertakings can be seen as part of the wider privatisation of US economy and technology development, which has been necessary as the wealthy have been subject to less taxation which funded such research in the past. This neoliberal model leaves the world's citizens with no democratic say or control over the technological programmes of the world's most sophisticated engineering groups. Today, a handful of Musks (and Bezoses, and Knights, and Jobses – plus a Zuckerberg for good measure) largely dictate the terms upon which the rest of us operate. The ability to harness such systems for one's own use is something that is almost impossible to control, given the lack of international regulation of finance.

Also, while there are scientific doubts about the actual viability of Mars colonisation, even regarding terrestrial plans for travelling at over 700 mph, Musk's new media projects are potentially closer to completion. He is concerned about the potential of AI, so maintains a foothold in that sector as well. In time, his organisation has created technology that can create fake news. While the intent was supposedly to study and control the potential problems of AI, even developing such a technology and making this publicly known can be a Pandora's box within the current political economy. Potentially-nefarious implications are more or less hand-delivered to those who would want to develop this technology to realise its darker functions (like social engineering).

(Continued)

(Continued)

While this may still seem like a far-off plan, we are reminded by Wade Rowland (2006) that the telegraph and pony express (a horse-based mail delivery system) once seemed like unbelievable ideas. By thinking ahead, even if the exact ideas do not happen, we are at least beginning to think and prepare for the world to come. Here and elsewhere, understanding the 'technology ideology' that underlies such plans will tell us much about their actual meaning, and potential uses. While some see Musk's vision as a harmonious and humanistic one, questions about ownership and control persist, and there may be very good reasons to start organising *against* such a future. Mechanisms such as Internet tracking technologies are already creating the foundation for this new world – indeed, this may simply be the terrifying final form of predictive analytics.

What do you think will be the future of new media? What technologies will our grandchildren use? How will you prepare for that? Think about both the utopic and dystopic possibilities of life in such a world.

....

....

....

....

....

....

....

....

....

....

....

....

....

....

The Final Word: Taking Your New Media Diet with a Grain of Salt

If you initially had a very enthusiastic attitude towards new media, this chapter may seem very negative. The point is not to discourage the use of new media internationally, but again, to encourage critical thinking about what it can and cannot actually do. Returning again to what we have learned in previous chapters, marketing can largely be thought of as a political game. It is an activity that requires a detailed and realistic understanding of your organisation's abilities and resources, as well as those of competitors. In new media contexts, we see the importance of **knowledge management** resources, in terms of personnel and partners who can engage in culturally specific and sensitive forms of **information-gathering**.

Readers are also cautioned to avoid simplistic narratives about new media use. In particular, it is important to keep in mind that new media are not necessarily cheaper, as older media often need to be used in tandem; as such, the costs may actually be additive or even multiplicative depending on the intensity and diversity of the international digital communications required. We also see that even easy new data gathering opportunities are not substitutes for traditional market research, as the voluminous new data is often not fit-for-purpose. Digital communications, meanwhile, may not be as deep, influential, or seemingly authentic as their old media predecessors.

Moreover, it should be noted that new media can bring with it new challenges. For example, research finds that new media is changing people's expectations of the speed of communications, which in turn is requiring a move towards 24/7 communications by organisations (and, in turn, consumers). Indeed, while we can magically transcend physical distance, this does not always mean we are 'in the same place' as those we are meeting. This can be a challenging feat, in terms of staffing (who wants to work the anti-trolling night shift on Twitter?!) and time zone differences. Here, and throughout, the inherent value of hiring local personnel should be apparent.

In short, many of the same principles of international marketing practice proposed throughout the book merit consideration here. Not only does the notion of marketing as politics still hold, but also many of the same political tactics and strategies required to compete effectively translate to new media spaces. Much the same work must be done, to prepare advertisements or engage in direct selling online. Issues of language, culture, and understanding more persist, generally unchanged. Globalisation, despite its clichéd image, has not brought us a world of homogeneity, but a world of continued diversity and ever-evolving demands.

8

Environmental Dystopia?

Figure 8.1   Our future?

Open almost any international marketing textbook or managerial guide, and you will find some section on sustainability. These vary from lip service to detailed guidance, but in all cases a fundamental question is sidestepped: is it not logically the case that international marketing would be inherently more carbon-intensive?

Think about it. The basic logic of traditional international marketing practice is that it is for some reason ideal for commerce to be occurring across long distances as much as possible.

The previous sections have shown us a number of reasons why this logic is problematic and unjust. In Chapter 1, we saw that the main reason why this is valuable is through the unjust division of labour, which has resulted from a series of complicated and long historical processes. In doing so, the autonomy and right to self-determination of people across the globe has been undermined in the name of a handful of corporations' right to privatise wealth... despite the fact that privatising wealth is the least productive use of capital. Elsewhere, under the topic of consumption, we saw that the styles and desires of those at the 'global centre' have often been imposed on others.

The topic of sustainability is going to be no different. It is yet another context wherein a certain logic of international marketing has been advanced by parties who benefit from it, and at great cost for a great many other people. Much as Usunier and Lee (2013) argued that America-centric models of global marketing are ideological, we also see that carbon intensive development has been promoted as necessary, when in reality this is an ideological claim. This perspective can be summarised in the following principles:

Principle 8a: Logically speaking, international marketing tends to be more carbon-intensive.

Principle 8b: This will increasingly become an issue in the era of climate change.

In supporting these arguments, I begin with reference to the latest scientific thinking on climate change. I keep this brief and do not entertain the notion that there is anything to 'debate' – at least where scientific matters are concerned – given the overwhelming consensus within scientific communities that it is real, serious, occurring now, and only increasing in severity (IPCC, 2018; Giddens, 2011; Pittock, 2009). This leaves more room for the *real* matters of debate – the social dimensions of this dilemma. In turning to these, I include some review of our past work on the subject, but focus mostly on more advanced theories from relevant fields, as well as new information about just how soon climate change is unfolding.

Throughout the chapter, we see the applicability of all of the 'New Foundations' yet again. I find that history is surprisingly informative, as looking to the past helps us understand how the carbon intensive economy came to be. We see that the normalisation of *unsustainability* was no accident, but a consciously-orchestrated affair. Then I introduce some key developments on ethics within this highly-politicised area of social life. The chapter ends with a new, Badiouian approach to climate change, focused on identifying the improbable but possible avenues for change. I illustrate this with a case from my own research on Toronto's local food scene.

Our Harrowing Future: The Burning Planet

In setting a baseline of scientific knowledge on climate change, I will start from the most recent statement on our grave climate future – the

United Nations International Panel on Climate Change's most recent report. Put simply, the Panel's report indicates that climate change is progressing faster than we could have ever imagined (IPCC, 2018). As has often been the case with IPCC reports (Pittock, 2009), scientists continue to discover new threats to the climate, which lead to multiplicative and even exponential changes to the rate of climate degradation in many contexts. New findings about the amount of carbon released as permafrost becomes... impermanent... are a good example here. As this is progressing at a rate far faster than expected, we are seeing a very large release of carbon from the natural environment, as well as unabated releases from human activities.

In short, things are even worse that we might think. The lukewarm (no pun intended) commitments of the Paris Climate Conference are seen to be not nearly enough, and moreover, the nations who signed up to it have not engaged in adequate actions in the time since to create the necessary changes. A minimum rise of 4 degrees Celsius is now seen to be inevitable, just operating at the levels of carbon emission we currently enjoy. This is absolutely catastrophic, with cities like New York and Miami at risk of being consumed by the ocean within decades, rather than a century. GDP of most developed countries, meanwhile, is expected to decrease by a minimum of 30 per cent... just from natural disasters alone. It remains to be seen how humans will react, and if we will engage in manmade disasters such as war, which may tear the world apart sooner than expected.

Now, more than ever, we see that climate change is absolutely happening. Almost every piece of scientific literature by credible climate scientists indicates that the situation is getting worse, on all measures. Climate change denial, meanwhile, is seen to be a patently indefensible position – simply an ideology promoted by those who want to continue in business unabated, despite what is happening around them (Washington and Cook, 2011; Craven, 2009; Hulme, 2009).

What We Know About Climate Change and Modern Capitalist Business Models

Climate change can be seen as one consequence of human activity in the **Anthropocene** – the time period within which humans have had a significant impact upon the climate and the Earth's processes. While Monbiot has noted that the sheer incursion of humans into ecosystems has had a warming effect (e.g. considering changes pre- and post-civilisation in Australia; 2016), the greatest effect has of course come when we made a regular practice of burning large amounts of fossil fuel. As explained by Andreas Malm (2016), modern capitalism was only possible through the use of **fossil capital** – the burning of cheap, easily harvested fossil fuels. For quite some time, the dangers of doing so were unknown, and during this time the consumer standards of countries like the United States were promoted as ideals towards which we should all work. The costs of this use, meanwhile, must be paid in the future, all while the energy resources required for even basic life – much less the largess of American mid-century consumerism – dwindle. The greenhouse effect was modelled in the 1960s and knowledge of climate change was easily accessible within scientific communities in the 1980s, but governments did not take scientists' grave pronouncements seriously (Giddens, 2011; Pittock, 2009). It seems that they were instead willing to bet that they might win in the battle for survival that would ensue.

We know that business, as it is conducted in the present, is not sustainable. Our supplies of many key resources are being depleted at an unconscionable rate. Comparatively more ecological changes tend to happen only when one of these resources disappears – for example, we saw the advent of compact fluorescent lighting when tungsten for traditional bulb filaments became too rare (Bloom, 2010).

At the same time, we remain wedded to an economy of not only continued productivity, but also economic growth. The need for growth began with the adoption of capitalism as the ideal model, as capital tends to rely on a financial class which expects to be paid back for any investment *with interest.* While some industries and value-adding activities are so excellent that this can be easily repaid, more often than not the physical and labour costs required bring enterprises close to the break-even point. More *cooperative* forms of banking and socio-economic organisation could improve this situation significantly.

There are real material limits to the growth economy. These were famously outlined long ago by E.F. Schumacher in the best-selling work of non-fiction called *Small Is Beautiful* (1973). It has been argued that perhaps new services and new media can be used to keep economies afloat, while reducing the need for real physical product production, but there are several problems with such arguments. First of all, digital technologies are not immaterial! All of our cloud services are based on servers, smartphones, laptops, and other physical media. Second, new technologies such as platforms tend to *increase concentration of ownership*, thereby decreasing the amount of value created and the number of individuals who can benefit from it.

Within international marketing, we see a couple of particularly problematic practices. The first is the **offshoring** of production, and the subsequent over-reliance on international shipping this requires.

This also tends to offshore pollution, which can make domestic stakeholders happy, but does not solve the global nature of the crisis. Here, we should be critical of arguments that countries like China are burning too much coal, when in reality they are doing so to support our own vicious consumer lifestyles! We should also be mindful that the waste produced *after* we are finished with these goods often ends up back in the developing world; developing countries, then, become responsible for the difficult and low-value work of trying to reclaim value from these near-worthless raw materials (Lora-Wainwright, 2017).

Acknowledging this, many business leaders continue to reject the notion of 'downshifting' or 'demarketing' as Kotler (2011) famously described it. A key example of how responsibility for preventing climate change is diffused was seen by the failure of the Kyoto Protocol. There, the United States never signed, and in turn many countries did not maintain their emissions reduction targets, as they argued doing so would be 'economic suicide' (Giddens, 2011). In short, they were at the mercy of the United States' poor ethical standards in order to remain competitive. Canada, for example, even *increased* their emissions during the timeframe.

Now, we have the Paris Climate Accord, and a new chance for international cooperation. We may only hope that the world has learned something from the Kyoto era, but it is very likely that it has not. This can be seen in the very weak positions taken in Paris, which will not come near what is required even if followed (IPCC, 2018).

Also of interest are questions concerning who is most responsible for emissions reductions in the present. Some argue that developing countries should make the greatest reductions, as they are often using carbon-intensive technologies, and as they have the opportunity to skip steps in their development. This is easier said than done, however, especially considering that these nations have considerably less economic capital with which to make these interventions. A counterargument is that it should actually be the developed nations who should make the greatest reductions, despite being hooked on incredibly carbon-intensive lifestyles (see Amstutz, 2018 for more on this debate). There, the point is that these countries have the privilege and technology required to do this – even if they do not have the popular will to do so.

Currently, many individual firms handle their sustainability missions through **corporate social responsibility (CSR)** policies, which communicate (at least intended) improvements in practices. Incorporating green values throughout a firm is seen as a way of reminding employees and customers alike of the importance of adopting green strategy. In stakeholder analysis, finally, companies may see those who are subject to pollution as stakeholders whose rights must be respected (see Banerjee,

2002 for more on this). All said, most countries have no legal obligation to engage in any of these practices, and as such they are simply not enough (Klein, 2014). In those that do, such as the Scandinavian countries, we still see a huge emphasis on investing in unsustainable operations in other countries (Witoszek and Midttun, 2018).

Contemporary Work on the Ethics of Climate Change

Most past work on ethics and sustainability has been haunted by arguments that their advice is not concrete or actionable. Still, there are things to be learned from this literature. I review this extant work in brief here, beginning with the actual ethics literature on the subject. This is surprisingly less incisive than work done by sociologists on the topic, so I cover that as well. While the 'ethics of climate change' discussion is long-standing, again from classics such as Schumacher's *Small Is Beautiful* (1973) and also Carson's *Silent Spring* (1962), I focus on contemporary discussions here, as they represent the most sophisticated thinking on the subject, and also provide the most contemporary explanation of the problem of sustainability.

Cripps (2013) provides what is arguably the most dedicated, philosophical exploration of sustainability ethics. This work focuses on each individual's ethical responsibility within this challenging social dilemma. The work is grounded in Kantian deontology, which you may remember from Chapter 2 is focused on the notion of duties. Being ethical, to Kant, was a miserable matter, made of doing not what is most pleasurable for you, but that which is best for society. Ultimately, such projects suffer from the sense that individuals all have a sort of equal or individual moral responsibility, rather than seeing one's choices about sustainability as being more structurally determined.

Other ethical approaches tend to draw upon politics and sociology a bit more. A good example is Vanderheiden's (2009) *Atmospheric Justice*, which draws on political philosophy and ethics. One concept brought in here is the notion of **intergenerational justice**. This concept is grounded in the altruism of Auguste Comte, who said that we each have a responsibility to future generations, as well as each other. Again, this falls into the trap of believing that each individual has a significant moral responsibility, when in reality many have little in the way of real ethical choice. Ironically, one could use the same argument to say that our ethics today are quite small, as they have largely been determined for us by those who came many generations beforehand.

Giddens' *The Politics of Climate Change* (2011), meanwhile, is arguably the best sociological work on climate ethics to date. There, he argues that sustainability is largely a 'chicken and egg' game, with consumers and everyday people blaming corporations for the poor state of the environment, and businesses claiming that customers simply won't pay for sustainability. In other words, he remains invested in the notion that 'both individuals and institutions' blame each other for the crisis (likely due to his allegiance to his own theory of structure vs. agency). A more realistic analysis might emphasise the role of institutions in creating the options and inaction of the masses.

Stevenson and Dryzek (2014), meanwhile, examine the issues of poor governance, which are widely acknowledged among sociopolitical accounts. There is, of course, generally poor leadership from government, regulatory agencies, and other powerful bodies on this matter. Their solution, however, has its own pitfalls. They recommend deliberative democracy, which we touched upon in Chapter 5 – which itself originates in the social theory of Jürgen Habermas. Their argument is that what is needed is more, and more meaningful, deliberation – that those affected by climate change should be brought into the discussion more. This is, and is not, true. On the one hand, we already have extensive knowledge of the misery that climate change inaction has brought to such parties. On the other hand, this information is not meaningfully incorporated into existing regulatory processes, which is the bigger problem. Still, the authors do not provide a very meaningful account of how we move from where we are *now* – where including such individuals is not considered an absolute requirement – to one in which their needs are magically the standard by which decisions are made.

Elsewhere, Mason (2015), Irwin (2001) and Beck (2016, 1995, 1992) address how a handful of powerful actors have organised society around a short-term approach through the notion of the '**risk society**', but they provide little insight into how this could be changed. Public intellectual, Naomi Klein (2014), provided an account of why climate change absolutely must be addressed, but lacks a clear sense of what actions are needed, or how they would come to pass.

A Badiouian Ethics of Combating Climate Change

I find that there is one more piece of the puzzle missing, and that it can actually be found within the humanities. Specifically, I find that the new ethical philosophy of Alain Badiou can be used to completely recast the most intractable of social problems – climate change included. While Badiou himself has demonstrated this broad applicability through his studies of French politics, the Arab Spring, and even the nature of love, it has yet to be extensively applied to climate change by any researcher.

Contemporaries of Badiou, who have similar analyses, have also not addressed the challenge. Žižek argues briefly that political inaction is produced through often inefficacious acts of 'conscious consumption' (2009), but does not provide an extensive analysis. Zygmunt Bauman (2009) comments on how the stresses of work and conspicuous consumption distract us from ethical deliberation, but also does not provide an extensive consideration of the implications for sustainability. Again, as seen in the previous section, works of philosophy from other traditions which have tried to address the topic remain wedded to the notion of individual responsibility, focused on 'each person doing what they can', rather than drawing our attention to the few individuals whose actions have the most impact. While the improbability of social change remains with a Badiouian perspective, this new philosophy is ultimately hopeful, as it argues that change can *only* occur once we have this sort of realistic analysis.

It would indicate that the notion of individual moral compasses on climate change ultimately distracts us from the true problems. In reality, climate change inaction is attributable to the fact that a few individuals have very large **moral compasses**; that they are pointed in the wrong direction; and that they sync the compasses of other social actors to their own. While small actions of lone individuals and small groups are better than none, we see that they will never add up to the change we need. To the small business owner or parent who just cannot understand how they can maintain the economic sustainability of their firms or their families while 'going green', there is an honest answer: it isn't possible, but that isn't your choice.

Case in Point

Food Sustainability in Toronto

Given all the reading I've done on sustainability, I find that I have no choice but to include this perspective into my research and teaching. As we've seen in this chapter, there's good reason for it, as climate change is already happening and will only accelerate in the future. This will have human consequences we should care about, as well as economic ones.

At the same time, I am troubled by some persistent problems within the business literature on sustainability. To begin, most of the key works emerged in the late 1990s and 2000s, followed by a larger societal trend of ignoring the environment for much of the time since. It seems that the recent new works cited here and the IPCC report may be bringing the matter into public consciousness again, but this has yet to trickle down into a similar surge of publications on sustainability. Perhaps more importantly, I found that the disciplines within which researchers worked tended to limit the scope of their studies. Consumer researchers studied consumers, while strategy and organisations researchers studied businesses, NGOs, and government. There wasn't anything that really captured an entire set of inter-related issues. Given the 'blinkers' which many business sustainability researchers seem to be wearing, it is perhaps needless to say that integration with other social science disciplines and the natural sciences was also lacking.

I found an approach which could do just that, so I wanted to see how it worked in practice. I started from Giddens' (2011) structuration approach, which is interested in the ways in which institutions and individuals shape each other, but also brought in the new Badiouian account of what that looks like in practice. This means that I take a very sceptical (more like realistic!) view of how much power all of us isolated individuals have – at least those of us who are not CEOs of Fortune 500 companies. Then I wanted to see who really did have the power, setting the terms by which everyone else operates. The idea from a Badiouian perspective is again to elucidate the ways in which the change needed could actually occur.

I chose the Toronto, Ontario local food scene as a site of investigation. There are several reasons for this. First, it is a hot spot for sustainable food production, with widespread public engagement on the issue. Second, Canada generally and Toronto specifically host a huge number of governmental, non-profit, and private organisations attempting to shape the nature of production and policy. Third, and building on these factors, the region has achieved a number of impressive objectives in terms

(Continued)

(Continued)

of scaling up sustainable food production (Friedmann, 2007), and thus a study of Toronto offers much for other municipalities and nations struggling with the same issues.

I was shocked by what I found! As noted in the paragraph above, Toronto is in many ways 'nailing it' on the sustainability front – at least compared to many other cities. Walk the streets and you will find no lack of cafes and shops which sell local, organic, and otherwise sustainably produced food – produce that has made it into both large retailers and small, dedicated shops. The town has a fairly 'crunchy' vibe with reasonable public engagement. And the NGOs I interviewed were engaging in some of the most innovative projects I've ever seen, pushing the boundaries of what was imaginable. The municipal government, for example, had a project of putting a local food farmers' market on a disused city bus and driving it to marginalised neighbourhoods where access to such goods was lacking – and in some cases, access to any fresh food was lacking (a phenomenon referred to as a **food desert**). At a local level, everything *seemed* to be coming up roses.

Then I interviewed officials at the national level. There, I found the Canadian government felt largely beholden to the whims of the *American public* – and by that, we generally mean *American business*. As Canada's economy depends on agriculture, and that is almost exclusively via trade with the much larger United States, there is a pressure to produce commodity-grade, uniform agricultural products for easy transport and identifiability. Hell, even the much-criticised, carbon intensive Alberta beef industry plays a more important role in policy, as the country has no choice but to let economic sustainability trump environmental sustainability. The pressures are so high that the Canadian government actually subsidises the big agricultural producers, which increases the cost of organic and sustainable food in the eyes of consumers. This helped me make new sense of the oft-cited crisis in that industry – that customers have no idea why it is so expensive compared to other food. It is not (entirely) attributable to its more expensive/less efficient mechanisms of production, but more determined by the fact that *unsustainable* agriculture was subsidised.

In time, I fed this back to my local participants. They found it to be troubling news – while they knew of the issues, they had not realised the scale in some cases, but perhaps more importantly matters of strategy had not been clear. In the paraphrased words of one interviewee who worked with a local sustainable food NGO: Does this mean that we should shut our doors and spend all of our time lobbying, since we're going to see nothing but small and potentially declining markets for sustainable food otherwise?

Perhaps! In cases like this, where it is the case that a handful of very powerful actors largely control the terms by which the rest of us act, there are questions about whether significant change can occur without systemic change. Indeed, political economy and sociological perspectives urge us to look at the complete picture, and where we see that current methods of resistance are labour-intensive but not working, there may be cause for a change of course.

The Final Word: Sustainability, from Here to the Future

Taking together the theories and case study presented in this chapter, I want to suggest a radical reconceptualisation of the notion of ethics. In the field of sustainability – and many others as well – I think it is most valuable to think of ethics and responsibility as dimensions of society, rather than individual life. In turn, different people have different levels of engagement and agency (the ability to change their own behaviour and that of others). Here and elsewhere, we live in a world where sadly a handful of powerful actors generally have the majority of the power. Where sustainability is concerned, this is unfortunately a cadre of 'unsustainability professionals'! As evidenced by the continued unsustainability of the food system (as a whole), these actors are not engaging in adequate environmentalist action, proportionate to the large ethical potential they hold. Making significant change within food economies (as seen above) or anywhere else will consequently require changing these actors' activities, one way or another.

While this may sound like a hopeless vision, we should be reminded that Badiouian analyses are meant to be hopeful. Badiou's assumption is that without a *realistic* idea of how things happen, there is no way to effectuate change upon them. Moreover, this helps us move away from profoundly unproductive modes of engagement. Consumer activism, for example, is unlikely to have the change we desire as so many are systematically barred from engaging in 'greener' behaviour (e.g. by low wages). Even small and medium sized enterprises often find themselves held hostage to the (often deplorable) ethical standards under which large multinationals operate. Ultimately, this sort of analysis helps us comparatively powerless people (unless you are Elon Musk... are you Elon Musk?) understand the situation in which they operate. As far as large, generally unsustainable actors are concerned, it shines a light on their misbehaviour, and discredits arguments that sustainability is 'not their responsibility'. By identifying governments (including international trade partners) and powerful businesses as the primary forces impeding sustainable development, the pathways by which sustainability could truly be *possible* are seen – even if such change is improbable.

Conclusion

You may wonder where to go, from what we have learned. There are many chapters in this book, and it can be hard to understand how they come together, much less how to weigh the various grave considerations which permeate the topics presented.

I suggest beginning with the environmental imperative, as it is the most pressing issue of our time. It is something that is likely to create the greatest disaster we have ever known, and to inhibit the viability of business – not to mention life! – itself.

Again, I find a Badiouian analysis useful here, and in considering much of international marketing practice. The point of such an analysis is to understand relative differences in power among relevant parties that interact within social space. As noted by Usunier and Lee and de Mooij, international marketing strategies are often based on fantasy and ideology, more than reality. Even if one wishes to indulge in the most crass business practice, understanding politics is essential, as the forms of knowledge and power that differentiate social actors largely determine what happens.

As far as actually coping with climate change and the new business world which we are all facing, there are a variety of solutions. The first is again to maintain faith to a realistic analysis, and hold the most powerful parties to account for this. We mustn't take on responsibilities we do not hold, either, as that only covers up problems. Indeed, the sense that we are in charge, when we really are not, has been actively created so as to promote a climate of inaction (we recycle each week in order to go on consuming). Importantly, this often means we only have power within our actions as citizens, rather than as businesspeople. For example, even if we are powerful within one contested domain of international marketing, this is unlikely to mean that we can change the behaviour of those in other industries.

In terms of international marketing, we must consider where it serves social good, and where re-localisation may be merited. And there is a reason for this, beyond simply reducing the carbon-intensity of our lives. This is also a matter of basic economic sustainability. In the present, we see a business environment where firms and countries do everything they can to sequester money within their own coffers, in a never-ending war against all others. Does this seem similar to anything else we have discussed? Possibly in Chapter 1?

Frankly, this is almost a form of mercantilism. We see countries financialising their economy and attempting to create self-interested trade regulations when in reality, much of their consumer expenditure (and hence potential tax revenue) is seeping out to all of the other countries doing the exact same things. We see cash flow and budget issues, declining real wages, and an inability for some services to compete. It is, if anything, an economic system without a ground.

At the same time, we must remember that the foundations of profit in much of international business are generally unjust, in and of themselves. It is a matter of basic human dignity to address these issues. This argument was perhaps best encapsulated by Che Guevara, in conversation with Italian novelist and intellectual, Italo Calvino:

Calvino: The European working class isn't interested in this talk about sacrifice. Or in the association of socialism with sacrifice and voluntary work. They are interested in cars and TV and higher wages. They support the Party because it leads the fight for higher wages. And they have a right to want this.

Che Guevara: I'm very happy for the European working class with their higher wages. But don't forget who is paying for those wages. We are – millions of exploited workers and peasants in Latin America, Africa and Asia. (quoted in Cope, 2015, location 1152)

In short, international marketing is a political game. It began with the enclosure of labour and resources as private, so that it could be traded for the creation of private wealth. Private wealth grows and becomes a greater and greater source of power, which is used to dictate the wages, resource values, and working conditions of those throughout the world. While we have largely naturalised this global division of labour, it is anything but natural.

Ultimately, the research and analyses presented in this textbook place you in an 'ethical situation', in the words of not only Badiou but also mainstream American marketing academics such as Sparks and Hunt (1998). You now know the real stakes of international marketing. To the degree to which you have power, you have responsibility. The choices you make have effects on others, and you now do so knowingly. So what will you do?

Appendix 1

Summary Workbook

A Place to Make *Your Own* Conclusions!

Unfortunately, that 'What will you do?' is not just a rhetorical question. The book doesn't end with me getting the final word, nor with an absurd, one-size-fits-all solution. I've got yet another set of questions for you on the pages that follow – and it's the longest yet! The idea is that they can help you summarise your thoughts here, so that you will be able to easily remember your impressions at a later date. You should answer them with your own vocation or interests in mind. Referring back to the new principles of international marketing may help in this exercise. I've gone ahead and collated them into a convenient summary in the Appendix that follows... aren't I kind?

What did you think international marketing was initially?

....

....

....

....

....

....

....

....

....

....

....

....

What do you think international marketing is now? If your views
have changed, how so? If they haven't, why not?

....

....

....

....

....

....

....

....

....

....

....

....

What sort of international marketing practice have you ordinarily
been interested in?

....

....

....

....

....

....

....

....

....

....

....

....

Are there important historical factors to consider in this sort of international marketing practice?

....

....

....

....

....

....

....

....

....

....

....

....

What aspects of your preferred industry (the one you work in, or hope to work in) might change, given the historical transformations we have seen previously?

....

....

....

....

....

....

....

....

....

....

....

....

What are the ethical stakes of the field of international marketing in which you are interested?

....
....
....
....
....
....
....
....
....
....
....
....

What are the politics (power dynamics) within this field? Do I actually have power and responsibility over standard practice, or am I subject to the power of others?

....
....
....
....
....
....
....
....
....
....
....
....

What international marketing models did you rely upon before
reading this book? Has your allegiance to them been altered
at all? If so, how?

....
....
....
....
....
....
....
....
....
....
....
....

In what ways can the fields of ethics, politics, and history enhance
your understanding of these models?

....
....
....
....
....
....
....
....
....
....
....
....

What about consumers? How do you think about them? What sorts of relationships do you try to produce? Are they 'healthy' ones?

....

....

....

....

....

....

....

....

....

....

....

....

What sort of practices do you engage in, when dealing with consumers?

....

....

....

....

....

....

....

....

....

....

....

....

Are you a merchant of culture? If so, how?

....
....
....
....
....
....
....
....
....
....
....
....

If not... how is it possible that what you do is completely 'acultural'?

....
....
....
....
....
....
....
....
....
....
....
....

Can the cultural dimension of my corner of international marketing create conflict or discomfort?

....

....

....

....

....

....

....

....

....

....

....

....

Are your market offerings from your own culture? If so, how can you avoid imposing your culture upon other cultures?

....

....

....

....

....

....

....

....

....

....

....

....

Alternatively, do you want to sell market offerings from a culture other than your own? If so, how can you honour those who provided intellectual property from which you profit? How do you negotiate these issues of ownership and appropriation?

....

....

....

....

....

....

....

....

....

....

....

....

Does new media actually improve the sort of international marketing that interests you? Or are there traditional barriers that persist?

....

....

....

....

....

....

....

....

....

....

....

....

Do new media technologies present new challenges and competition as well?

....
....
....
....
....
....
....
....
....
....
....
....

How sustainable are the industries that you are interested in?

....
....
....
....
....
....
....
....
....
....
....
....

What power do you have to create a sustainable future within those industries? And more generally?

....

....

....

....

....

....

....

....

....

....

....

....

Appendix 2

New Principles of International Marketing

Principle 1: The composition, dynamics, and practices of contemporary international marketing are largely shaped by historical relationships and processes.

Principle 2: The ethical stakes of international marketing are often hidden, complicated, and difficult to impact – but comprehending ethics is nevertheless crucial for understanding international marketing practice.

Principle 3: As international marketing is an exercise of power, it is inherently political.

Principle 4a: While internationalisation is often considered inherently valuable as it can increase economy of scale, it is not a guaranteed route to profitability. It depends on the context, resources, and strategies of the firm.

Principle 4b: The most powerful players within a set of interconnected international marketers generally set the terms by which everyone else must play.

Principle 5a: Our understanding of consumer culture can be improved by thinking of it as a system produced in specific times and places, for the purpose of maximising the production of wealth.

Principle 5b: 'Being a consumer' is best understood as an obligation produced by consumer culture, which makes individuals believe that they are personally responsible for their success (or failure) within this complicated political system.

Principle 5c: While international consumer research texts often urge a careful consideration of local culture, a historical and political model reveals how many firms can avoid doing this work through brute force strategies such as establishing de facto monopolies, rather than winning customers by consent.

Principle 5d: The ethical and political dimensions of consumption are better conceptualised as collectively and sociologically determined rather than individual.

Principle 6a: As all modern nations are multicultural in some way or another, intercultural marketing principles have domestic as well as international applications.

Principle 6b: The 'international-ness' (or culturally defined character) of a product is often what makes it of value outside of its context of origin.

Principle 6c: The evolution of what is valuable culture over time can be best understood as a historical process – specifically, one where powerful cultures have imposed their standards upon others.

Principle 7a: In identifying the role of new media in international marketing practice, it is essential to separate our beliefs from reality.

Principle 7b: While new media have special benefits (e.g. decreasing the cost and timeline of international communications), many of the same principles of marketing and communications apply to these media as well.

Principle 8a: Logically speaking, international marketing tends to be more carbon-intensive.

Principle 8b: This will increasingly become an issue in the era of climate change.

Recommended Reading

A handful of books I would recommend, to learn more about the topics covered in this book:

Amin, Samir (2014 [1997]) *Capitalism in the Age of Globalization.*
Badiou, Alain (2001) *Ethics.*
Cope, Zak (2015) *Divided World, Divided Class.*
Dahl, Robert A. and Bruce Stinebrickner (2002) *Modern Political Analysis.*
Giddens, Anthony (2011) *The Politics of Climate Change.*
Parenti, Michael (2011) *The Face of Imperialism.*
Pilcher, Jeffrey (2012) *Planet Taco.*
Robinson, David and Chris Garratt (2008) *Introducing Ethics: A Graphic Guide.*
Said, Edward (1994) *Culture and Imperialism.*
Sunstein, Cass (2018) *#republic.*

References

Abecassis-Moedas, C. (2007) 'Globalisation and Regionalisation in the Clothing Industry: Survival Strategies for UK Firms', *International Journal of Entrepreneurship and Small Business*, 4(3): 291–304.

Ackland, C. (2012) *Swift Viewing: The Popular Life of Subliminal Influence*. Durham, NC: Duke University Press.

Agamben, G. (2009) *What Is an Apparatus?: And Other Essays*. Stanford, CA: Stanford University Press.

Agamben, G. (2004) *The Open: Man and Animal*. Stanford, CA: Stanford University Press.

Agamben, G. (1999) *Homo Sacer: Sovereign Power and Bare Life*. Stanford, CA: Stanford University Press.

Alamgir, F. and Banerjee, S.B. (2019) 'Contested Compliance Regimes in Global Production Networks: Insights from the Bangladesh Garment Industry', *Human Relations*, 72(2): 272–297.

Ali, T. (2018) *The Extreme Centre: A Second Warning*. London: Verso.

Amin, S. (2014 [1997]) *Capitalism in the Age of Globalization*. London: Zed.

Amstutz, M.R. (2018) *International Ethics: Concepts, Theories and Cases in Global Politics* (5th edn). Lanham, MA: Rowman & Littlefield.

Aronowitz, S. (2001) *The Knowledge Factory: Dismantling the Corporate University and Creating True Higher Learning*. Boston, MA: Beacon Press.

Ash, L. (2012) 'London, France's Sixth Biggest City', *BBC News*. Online edition, 30 May. Available at: https://www.bbc.co.uk/news/magazine-18234930 (accessed 8 February 2019).

Ashby, C. (2016) *Modernism in Scandinavia: Art, Architecture and Design*. London: Bloomsbury.

Asimov, I. (1980) *In Joy Still Felt: The Autobiography of Isaac Asimov 1954–1978*. New York: Doubleday.

Askegaard, S. and Linnet, J.T. (2011) 'Towards an Epistemology of Consumer Culture Theory: Phenomenology and the Context of Context', *Marketing Theory*, 11 (December): 381–404.

Baack, D.W., Harris, E.G. and Baack D.E. (2018) *International Marketing*. London: Sage.

Badiou, A. (2001) *Ethics*. London: Verso.

Banerjee, S.B. (2017) 'Contested Compliance Regimes'. Lecture at the University of Leicester.

Banerjee, S.B. (2002) 'Corporate Environmentalism: The Construct and Its Measurement', *Journal of Business Research*, 55(3): 177–191.

Bartels, R. (1976) *The History of Marketing Thought* (2nd edn). Columbus, OH: Publishing Horizons.

Barthes, R. (1967) *The Fashion System*. Berkeley, CA: University of California Press.

Bauman, Z. (2013) *Collateral Damage: Social Inequalities in a Global Age*. Cambridge: Polity.

Bauman, Z. (2009) *Does Ethics Have a Chance in a World of Consumers?* Cambridge, MA: Harvard University Press.

BBC (2018b) 'Reality Check: Does UK Spend Half as Much on Health as US?', Published: February 6, 2018. Available at: https://www.bbc.com/news/uk-42950587 (accessed 20 March 2019).

BBC (2018a) 'M&S Outsources Half of its Tech Jobs', *BBC News*. Online edition, 9 January 2018. Available at: https://www.bbc.co.uk/news/business-42629522 (accessed 8 February 2019).

Beck, U. (2016) *The Metamorphosis of the World: How Climate Change Is Transforming Our Concept of the World*. Cambridge: Polity.

Beck, U. (1995) *Ecological Enlightenment: Essays On The Politics Of The Risk Society*. Atlantic Highlands, NJ: Humanities Press.

Beck, U. (1992) *Risk Society: Towards a New Modernity*. London: Sage.

Beverland, M.B. and Farrelly, F.J. (2009) 'The Quest for Authenticity in Consumption: Consumers' Purposive Choice of Authentic Cues to Shape Experienced Outcomes', *Journal of Consumer Research*, 36 (February): 838–856.

Bloom, A.J. (2010) *Global Climate Change: Convergence of Disciplines*. Sunderland, MA: Sinauer Associates.

Bocock, R. (1993) *Consumption*. London: Routledge.

Bradshaw, A. (2013) '"Bringing With Us the Plague": Consumer Research as Machinery of Zoomorphism', *Journal of Marketing Management*, 29(1–2): 249–262.

Brewer, M.B. and Chen, Y.-R. (2007) 'Where (Who) Are Collectives in Collectivism? Toward Conceptual Clarification of Individualism and Collectivism', *Psychological Review*, 114(1): 133–151.

Brunnström, L. (2018) *Swedish Design: A History*. London: Bloomsbury.

Buckingham, D. (2003) *Media Education: Literacy, Learning and Contemporary Culture*. Cambridge: Polity.

Bukharin, N. (1987 [1929]) *Imperialism and World Economy*. London: Merlin Press.

Burton, D. and Klemm, M. (2011) 'Whiteness, Ethnic Minorities and Advertising in Travel Brochures', *The Service Industries Journal*, 31(5): 679–693.

Butler, S. (2016) 'Tesco Delayed Payments to Suppliers to Boost Profits, Watchdog Finds', *The Guardian*. Online edition, 26 January. Available at: https://www.theguardian.com/business/2016/jan/26/tesco-ordered-change-deal-suppliers (accessed 8 February 2019).

Butler, S. (2013) 'Tesco Accused of Squeezing Suppliers to Support Its Profits', *The Guardian*. Online edition, 28 November. Available at: https://www.theguardian.com/business/2013/nov/28/tesco-accused-of-squeezing-suppliers (accessed 8 February 2019).

Byrne, D. (1999) 'I Hate World Music', *The New York Times*, 3 October. Available at: https://archive.nytimes.com/query.nytimes.com/gst/fullpage-9901EED8163EF930A35753C1A96F958260.html (accessed 8 February 2019).

Cahn, Z. and Siegel, M. (2011) 'Electronic Cigarettes as Harm Reduction Strategy for Tobacco Control: A Step Forward, or a Repeat of Past Mistakes?', *Journal of Public Health Policy*, 32(1): 16–31.

Carruthers, B. and Babb, S.L. (2013) *Economy/Society: Markets, Meanings, and Social Structure*. London: Sage.

Carson, R. (1962) *Silent Spring*. Boston, MA: Houghton Mifflin.

Cassels, J.M. (1936) 'The Significance of Early Economic Thought on Marketing', *Journal of Marketing*, 1(2): 129–133.

Chapman, P. (2009) *Bananas: How the United Fruit Company Shaped the World*. New York, NY: Canongate.

Cherry, M. (2016) 'Virtual Work and Invisible Labor', in M. Crain, W. Poster and M. Cherry (eds), *Invisible Labor: Hidden Work in the Contemporary World*. Berkeley, CA: University of California Press, pp. 71–86.

Cialdini, R.B. (2009) *Influence: The Psychology of Persuasion*. New York: William Morrow and Company.

Claus , P. and Mariott, J. (2012) *History: An Introduction to Theory, Method and Practice* (2nd edn). New York: Routledge.

Clements, J.D. (2014) *Corporations Are Not People: Reclaiming Democracy from Big Money and Global Corporations*. San Francisco, CA: Berrett-Koehler.

Clunas, C. (2004) *Superfluous Things: Material Culture and Social Status in Early Modern China*. Honolulu: University of Hawaii Press.

Cohen, L. (2003) *A Consumer's Republic*. New York: Knopf.

Colvin, J. (2017) 'Trump Says He Doesn't Trust Computers As He Rings in 2017', *Associated Press News*. Online edition, 1 January. Available at: https://apnews.com/3cc7e56c71bc49978823ce54f318f6cd (accessed 8 February 2019).

Coolsen, F.G. (1960) *Marketing Thought in the United States in the Late Nineteenth Century*. Lubbock: Texas Tech Press.

Cope, Z. (2015) *Divided World, Divided Class: Global Political Economy and the Stratification of Labour Under Capitalism* (2nd edn). Montreal: Kersplebedeb.

Costanza-Chock, S. (2012) 'Mic Check! Media Cultures and the Occupy Movement', *Social Movement Studies: Journal of Social, Cultural and Political Protest*, 11(3–4): 375–385.

Craig, E. (2002) *Philosophy: A Very Short Introduction*. Oxford: Oxford University Press.

Craven, G. (2009) *What's the Worst that Could Happen? A Rational Response to the Climate Change Debate*. New York: Perigee.

Cripps, E. (2013) *Climate Change and the Moral Agent: Individual Duties in an Interdependent World*. Oxford: Oxford University Press.

Czinkota, M.R., Ronkainen, I. and Zvobgo, G. (2011) *International Marketing*. Andover: Cengage.

Dahl, R.A. and Stinebrickner, B. (2002) *Modern Political Analysis* (6th edn). Harlow: Pearson.

Dahl, R.A. (1970) *Modern Political Analysis*. NewYork: Prentice-Hall.

Dahl, S. (2018) *Social Media Marketing: Theories and Applications*. London: Sage.

Davenport, C. (2018) *The Space Barons: Elon Musk, Jeff Bezos, and the Quest to Colonize the Cosmos*. New York: Hachette.

Davis, R.C. and Marvin, G.R. (2004) *Venice, the Tourist Maze: A Cultural Critique of the World's Most Touristed City*. Berkeley, CA: University of California Press.

Delfanti, A. and Arvidsson, A. (2019) *Introduction to Digital Media*. Hoboken, NJ: Wiley.

de Mooij, M. (2019) *Global Marketing and Advertising: Understanding Cultural Paradoxes*. Thousand Oaks, CA: Sage.

DiMaggio, P.J. and Powell, W.W. (2012) 'Introduction', in W.W. Powell and P.J. DiMaggio (eds), *The New Institutionalism in Organizational Analysis*. Chicago: University of Chicago, pp. 1–40.

Dobers, P. and Hallin, A. (2009) 'The Use of Internet in Building the Brand of "Stockholm: The Capital of Scandinavia"', in Mila Gasco-Hernandez and Teresa Torres-Coronas (eds), *Information Communication Technologies and City Marketing: Digital Opportunities for Cities Around the World*. Hershey, PA: Information Science Reference, pp. 265–294.

Dorfman, A. (2009) *The Empire's Old Clothes: What the Lone Ranger, Babar and Other Innocent Heroes Do to Our Minds*. Durham, NC: Duke University Press.

Dorfman, A. and Mattelart, A. (2019 [1971]) *How to Read Donald Duck: Imperialist Ideology in the Disney Comic*. London: Pluto Press.

Duhigg, C. (2018) 'Dr. Elon & Mr.Musk: Life Inside Tesla's Production Hell', *Wired*. Online edition, 13 December. Available at: https://www.wired.com/story/elon-musk-tesla-life-inside-gigafactory/ (accessed 8 February 2019).

Duhigg, C. (2012) 'How Companies Learn your Secrets', *The New York Times Magazine*, 16 February. Available at: https://www.nytimes.com/2012/02/19/magazine/shopping-habits.html (accessed 8 February 2019).

Dyer-Witherford, N. (2015) *Cyber-Proletariat: Global Labour in the Digital Vortex*. London: Pluto Press.

Eagle, L. and Dahl, S. (2015) *Marketing Ethics & Society*. London: Sage.

Egan, J. (2014) *Marketing Communications*. London: Sage.

Eisenhardt, K. M. and Bourgeois, L. J. (1988) 'Politics of Strategic Decision Making in High-Velocity Environments: Toward a Midrange Theory', *Academy of Management Journal*, 31(4): 737–770.

El-Ansary, A.I. and Stern, L.W. (1972) 'Power Measurement in the Distribution Channel', *Journal of Marketing Research*, 9 (February): 47–52.

Ellis, N., Fitchett, J., Higgins, M., Jack, G., Lim, M., Saren, M. and Tadajewski, M. (2011) *Marketing: A Critical Textbook*. London: Sage.

England, C. (2017) 'Supermarkets Using 'Shocking Tactics' to Extract Money from Suppliers', *The Independent*. Online edition, 12 March. Available at: https://www.independent.co.uk/news/uk/home-news/supermarkets-using-shocking-tactics-to-extract-money-from-suppliers-a7625936.html (accessed 8 February 2019).

Escobar, A. (2018) *Designs for the Pluriverse: Radical Interdependence, Autonomy and the Making of Worlds*. Durham, NC: Duke University Press.

Fairclough, N. (2014) *Language and Power* (3rd edn). London: Routledge.

Fairclough, N. (2003) *Analysing Discourse: Textual Analysis for Social Research*. London: Routledge.

Featherstone, M. (2007) *Consumer Culture and Postmodernism* (2nd edn). London: Sage.

Ferraris, M. (2015) *Manifesto for New Realism*. Albany, NY: SUNY Press.

Ferraris, M. (2014) *Introduction to New Realism*. London: Bloomsbury.

Ferraris, M. (2012) *Manifesto for New Realism* (S. De Sanctis, trans.). Albany, NY: SUNY Press

Fiell, C. and Fiell, P. (2013) *Scandinavian Design*. Cologne: Taschen.

Fill, C. and Turnbull, S. (2016) *Marketing Communications: Discovery, Creation and Conversations*. London: Pearson.

Firat, A.F. and Dholakia, N. (1998) *Consuming People: From Political Economy to Theatres of Consumption*. London: Routledge.

Fournier, S. (1998) 'Consumers and Their Brands: Developing Relationship Theory in Consumer Research', *Journal of Consumer Research*, 24(4): 343–373.

Freeman, R.E. (1994) 'The Politics of Stakeholder Theory: Some Future Directions', *Business Ethics Quarterly*, 4 (October): 409–421.

Friedmann, H. (2007), 'Scaling Up: Bringing Public Institutions and Food Service Corporations into the Project For a Local, Sustainable Food System in Ontario', *Agriculture and Human Values*, 24(3): 389–398.

Fuchs, C. (2017) *Social Media: A Critical Introduction*. London: Sage.

Gabbatiss, J. (2018) 'Carbon Emissions from Global Shipping to be Halved by 2050, Says IMO', *The Independent*. Online edition, 13 April. Available at: https://www.independent.co.uk/environment/ships-emissions-carbon-dioxide-pollution-shipping-imo-climate-change-a8303161.html (accessed 8 February 2019).

Galbraith, J.K. (2004) *The Economics of Innocent Fraud: Truth for Our Time*. New York: Penguin.

Ganesan, S. (1994) 'Determinants of Long-Term Orientation in Buyer–Seller Relationships', *Journal of Marketing*, 58(2): 1–19.

Gaski, J.F. (1984) 'The Theory of Power and Conflict in Channels of Distribution', *Journal of Marketing*, 48 (Summer): 9–29.

Gaski, J.F. and Nevin, J.R. (1985) 'The Differential Effects of Exercised and Unexamined Power Sources in a Marketing Channel', *Journal of Marketing Research*, 22 (May): 130–142.

Giddens, A. (2011) *The Politics of Climate Change*. Cambridge: Polity.

Giesler, M. and Veresiu, E. (2014) 'Creating the Responsible Consumer: Moralistic Governance Regimes and Consumer Subjectivity', *Journal of Consumer Research*, 41(3): 840–857.

Gilmore, J.H. and Pine, B.J. (2007) *Authenticity: What Consumers Really Want*. Cambridge, MA: Harvard Business Review Press.

Ginzburg, C. (1999) *The Judge and the Historian: Marginal Notes and a Late Twentieth-Century Miscarriage of Justice*. London: Verso.

Gostin, L.O. and Glasner, A.Y. (2014) 'E-Cigarettes, Vaping, and Youth', *Journal of the American Medical Association*, 312(6): 595–596.

Graeber, D. (2013) *The Democracy Project*. New York: Penguin.

Gramsci, A. (1929–1935) *Prison Notebooks*. New York: International Publishers.

Griffiths, K. (2018) 'Outsourcing is Latest Tech Idea at M&S', *The Times*, Online edition, 10 January. Available at: https://www.thetimes.co.uk/article/outsourcing-is-latest-tech-idea-at-m-s-5qmp67b96 (accessed 8 February 2019).

Gromark, J. (2017) 'Stockholm: The Narcissistic Capital of Scandinavia', in M. Karavatzis, M. Giovanardi, and M. Lichrou (eds), *Inclusive*

Place Branding: Critical Perspectives on Theory and Practice. London: Routledge.

Gunn, S. (2006) *History and Cultural Theory*. Harlow: Pearson.

Gurman, T.A., Rubin, S.E. and Roess, A.A. (2012) 'Effectiveness of Health Behavior Change Communication Interventions in Developing Countries: A Systematic Review of the Literature', *Journal of Health Communication*, 17 (supplement 1): 82–104.

Habermas, J. (1989 [1962]) *The Structural Transformation of the Public Sphere: An Inquiry into a Category of Bourgeois Society*. Cambridge, MA: MIT Press.

Hackley, C. and Hackley, R.A. (2017) *Advertising and Promotion* (4th edn). London: Sage.

Hall, S. (1997) *Representation: Cultural Representations and Signifying Practices*. London: Sage.

Hallward, P. (2001) 'Introduction', in A. Badiou (ed.), *Ethics*. London: Verso, pp. vii–xlviii.

Harvey, D. (2005) *The New Imperialism*. Oxford: Oxford University Press.

Hebdige, D. (1979) *Subculture: The Meaning of Style*. London: Routledge.

Hickell, J. (2018) *The Divide: A Brief Guide to Global Inequality and Its Solutions*. New York: Penguin.

Ho, K. (2009) *Liquidated: An Ethnography of Wall Street*. Durham, NC: Duke University Press.

Hofstede, G. (1983) 'Culture's Consequences: International Differences in Work-related Values', Administrative Science Quarterly 28(4): 625–629.

Hoogvelt, A. (2001) *Globalization and the Postcolonial World: The New Political Economy of Development*. Baltimore, MD: Johns Hopkins University Press.

Horkheimer, M. and Adorno, T.W. (1947/1972) *Dialectic of Enlightenment*. New York: Continuum.

Howard, J.A. and Sheth, J. (1969) 'The Theory of Buyer Behavior', *Journal of the American Statistical Association*, 467–487.

Howell, M. and Prevenier, W. (2001) *From Reliable Sources: An Introduction to Historical Methods*. Ithaca, NY: Cornell University Press.

Hulme, M. (2009) *Why We Disagree About Climate Change: Understanding Controversy, Inaction and Opportunity*. Cambridge: Cambridge University Press.

Humphreys, A. (2010) 'Semiotic Structure and the Legitimation of Consumption Practices: The Case of Casino Gambling', *Journal of Consumer Research*, 37 (October): 490–510.

Hunt, S.D. and Morgan, R.M. (1995) 'The Comparative Advantage Theory of Competition', *Journal of Marketing*, 59 (April): 1–15.

Hunt, S.D. and Nevin, J.R. (1974) 'Power in a Channel of Distribution: Sources and Consequences', *Journal of Marketing Research*, 11 (May): 186–193.

Iainniciello, C. (2018) *Migrations, Arts and Postcoloniality in the Mediterranean*. London: Routledge.

IPCC (International Panel on Climate Change) (2018) *Global Warming of 1.5 °C: An IPCC Special Report*. Geneva: IPCC. Available at: www.ipcc.ch/sr15/ (accessed 8 February 2019).

Irwin, A. (2001) *Sociology and the Environment: A Critical Introduction to Society, Nature and Knowledge*. Cambridge: Polity.

Isherwood, J. and Litterick, D. (2007) 'McDonald's Accused of Piracy by Chair Firm', *The Telegraph*. Online edition, 9 October. Available at: https://www.telegraph.co.uk/finance/markets/2817421/McDonalds-accused-of-piracy-by-chair-firm.html (accessed 8 February 2019).

Izberk-Bilgin, E. (2012) 'Infidel Brands: Unveiling Alternative Meanings of Global Brands at the Nexus of Globalization, Consumer Culture and Islamism', *Journal of Consumer Research*, 39(4): 663–687.

Jandt, F.E. (2013) *An Introduction to Intercultural Communication* (7th edn). London: Sage.

Jones, B.D.G. and Shaw, E.H. (2006) 'A History of Marketing Thought', in B. Weitz and R. Wensley (eds), *Handbook of Marketing*. London: Sage, pp. 39–65.

Jones, C., ten Bos, R. and Parker, M. (2005) *For Business Ethics*. Abingdon: Routledge.

Kelley, W.T. (1956) 'The Development of Early Thought in Marketing and Production', *Journal of Marketing*, 21(1): 62–67.

Keynes, J.M. (1936) *The General Theory of Employment, Interest and Money*. London: Palgrave.

Khan, O. (2005) 'Risk in the Textile Industry: The Case of Marks and Spencer', *EThOS*: E-Theses Online Service (British Library). PhD Thesis, Manchester Business School.

Klein, N. (2014) *This Changes Everything: Capitalism vs. the Climate*. New York: Penguin.

Kotler, P. (2011) 'Reinventing Marketing to Manage the Environmental Imperative', *Journal of Marketing*, 75 (July): 132–135.

Kotler, P. (1980) *Principles of Marketing*. Harlow: Pearson.

Kotler, P. and Armstrong, G. (2017) *Principles of Marketing* (17th edn, Global Edition). Harlow: Pearson.

Kotler, P. and Levy, S.J. (1969) 'Broadening the Concept of Marketing', *Journal of Marketing*, 36 (April): 46–54.

Krishna, S., Boren, S.A. and Balas, E.A. (2009) 'Healthcare via Cell Phones: A Systematic Review', *Telemedicine and e-Health*, 15(3): 231–240.

Lasswell, H.D. (1936) *Politics: Who Gets What, When, and How*. New York: McGraw-Hill.

Lazzarato, M. (2015) *Governing by Debt*. Los Angeles, CA: Semiotext(e).

Lazzarato, M. (2012) *The Making of the Indebted Man*. Los Angeles, CA: Semiotext(e).

Leiss, W., Kline, S., Jhally, S. and Botterill, J. (2018) *Social Communication in Advertising* (4th edn). Abingdon: Taylor & Francis.

Levinson, M. (2016) *The Box: How the Shipping Container Made the World Smaller and the World Economy Bigger* (2nd edn). Princeton, NJ: Princeton University Press.

Lopatto, E. (2018) 'What Tesla's Union-Busting Trial Means for the Rest of Silicon Valley', *The Verge*, 29 September. Available at: https://www.theverge.com/2018/9/29/17914572/tesla-union-trial-silicon-valley-unionization-elon-musk (accessed 8 February 2019).

Lora-Wainwright, A. (2017) *Resigned Activism: Living with Pollution in Rural China*. Cambridge, MA: MIT Press.

Macdonald, S. (2013) *Memorylands: Heritage and Identity in Europe Today*. Abingdon: Routledge.

MacMillan, M. (2010) *The Uses and Abuses of History*. London: Profile.

Malm, A. (2016) *Fossil Capital: The Rise of Steam Power and the Roots of Global Warming*. London: Verso.

Malthus, T.R. (1798) *An Essay on the Principle of Population*. London: J. Johnson.

Marazzi, C. (2011) *The Violence of Financial Capitalism*. Los Angeles, CA: Semiotext(e).

Marshall, A. (1890) *Principles of Economics*. London: Macmillan.

Marx, K. (1990 [1867]) *Capital*, Vol. 1. New York: Penguin.

Marx, K. and Engels, F. (1848) *The Communist Manifesto*. London: The Communist League.

Mason, P. (2015) *Postcapitalism: A Guide to Our Future*. New York: Penguin.

McClintock, A. (1994) *Soft-Soaping Empire: Commodity Racism and Imperial Advertising*. London: Routledge.

McCracken, G. (1986) 'Culture and Consumption: A Theoretical Account of the Structure and Movement of the Cultural Meaning of Consumer Goods', *Journal of Consumer Research*, *13*(1): 71–84.

McKenzie, H. (2018) *Insane Mode: How Elon Musk's Tesla Sparked an Electric Revolution to End the Age of Oil: Inside Tesla and Elon Musk's Mission to Save the World*. London: Faber & Faber.

McSweeney, B. (2002) 'Hofstede's Model of National Cultural Differences and their Consequences: A Triumph of Faith – a Failure of Analysis', *Human Relations*, *55*(1): 89–118.

Menon, A., Bharadwaj, S.G., Adidam, P.T. and Edison, S.W. (1999) 'Antecedents and Consequences of Marketing Strategy Making', *Journal of Marketing*, 63(2): 18–40.

Merchant, B. (2017) 'Life and Death in Apple's Forbidden City', *The Observer*. Online edition, 18 June. Available at: https://www.theguardian.com/technology/2017/jun/18/foxconn-life-death-forbidden-city-longhua-suicide-apple-iphone-brian-merchant-one-device-extract (accessed 8 February 2019).

Mihalidis, P. (2018) *Civic Media Literacies: Re-Imagining Human Connection in an Age of Digital Abundance*. New York: Peter Lang.

Mihalidis, P. (2014) *Media Literacy and the Emerging Citizen: Youth, Engagement and Participation in Digital Culture*. New York: Peter Lang.

Mintz, S.W. (1985) *Sweetness and Power: The Place of Sugar in Modern History*. London: Penguin.

Monbiot, G. (2016) *How Did We Get into This Mess?* London: Verso.

Mosco, V. (2009) *The Political Economy of Communications* (2nd edn). London: Sage.

Moulds, J. (2015) 'Supermarkets Behaving Badly – How Suppliers Can Get a Fairer Deal', *The Guardian*. Online edition, 25 June. Available at: https://www.theguardian.com/small-business-network/2015/jun/25/tesco-supermarkets-behaving-badly-suppliers (accessed 8 February 2019).

Murphy, K.M. (2015) *Swedish Design: An Ethnography*. Ithaca, NY: Cornell University Press.

Niazi, T. (2005) 'Global Inaction, Ethnic Animosity, or Resource Maldistribution? An Ecological Explanation for Genocide in Rwanda', in G.C. Kinloch and R.P. Mohan (eds), *Genocide: Approaches, Case Studies, and Responses*. New York: Algora Publishing, pp. 163–194.

Norman, D. (1988) *The Psychology of Everyday Things*. New York: Basic Books.

Now This! (2017) 'Meet the Woman Who Wants to Save the World', 27 September. Available online at: https://nowthisnews.com/videos/her/melinda-gates-is-saving-the-world-and-fighting-for-womens-rights (accessed 8 February 2019).

Ozanne, J.L., Corus, C. and Saatcioglu, B. (2009) 'The Philosophy and Methods of Deliberative Democracy: Implications for Public Policy and Marketing', *Journal of Public Policy & Marketing*, 28(1): 29–40.

Palmer, G. (2009) *The Politics of Breastfeeding: When breasts are bad for business*. London: Pinter & Martin.

Papacharissi, Z. (2011) *A Private Sphere: Democracy in a Digital Age*. Cambridge: Polity.

Parenti, M. (2011) *The Face of Imperialism*. London: Routledge.

Perlmutter, H.V. (1969) 'The Torturous Evolution of the Multinational Corporation', *Columbia Journal of World Business*, 4(1): 8–18.

Pilcher, J.M. (2012) *Planet Taco: A Global History of Mexican Food*. Oxford: Oxford University Press.

Pittock, A.B. (2009) *Climate Change: The Science, Impacts and Solutions*. Abingdon: Earthscan.

Platteau, J.P. and Abraham, A. (2002) 'Participatory Development in the Presence of Endogenous Community Imperfections', *Journal of Development Studies*, 39(2): 104–136.

Porter, M.E. (2008) 'The Five Competitive Forces that Shape Strategy', *Harvard Business Review*, 86(1): 57–71.

Porter, M.E. (1979) 'How Competitive Forces Shape Strategy', *Harvard Business Review*, 57(2): 137–145.

Rahman, S. (2013) *Broken Promises of Globalization: The Case of the Bangladesh Garment Industry*. Plymouth: Lexington Books.

Rappaport, E. (2015) 'Drink Empire Tea: Gender, Conservative Politics and Imperial Consumerism in Inter-War Britain', in E. Rappaport, S. Trudgen Dawson and M.J. Crowley (eds), *Consuming Behaviours: Identity, Politics and Pleasure in Twentieth-Century Britain*. London: Bloomsbury: 139–158.

Rancière, J. (1995) *On the Shores of Politics*. London: Verso.

Rassuli, K. and Hollander, S.C. (1986) 'Desire – Induced, Innate, Insatiable?', *Journal of Macromarketing*, 6 (Fall): 4–24.

Raven, B.H. (1965) 'Social Influence and Power', in I.D. Steiner and M. Fishbein (eds), *Current Studies in Social Psychology*. New York: Holt, Rinehart, Winston, pp. 371–382.

Ravi, B.K. (2017) *Modern Media, Elections, and Democracy*. London: Sage.

Richins, M.L. (2011) 'Materialism, Transformation Expectations, and Spending: Implications for Credit Use', *Journal of Public Policy & Marketing*, 30(2): 141–156.

Richins, M.L. (1994) 'Special Possessions and the Expression of Material Values', *Journal of Consumer Research*, 21(3): 522–533.

Rindfleisch, A. and Heide, J.B. (1997) 'Transaction Cost Analysis: Past, Present and Future Applications', *Journal of Marketing*, 61 (October): 30–54.

Roberts, S.T. (2017) 'Content Moderation', in L.A. Schintler and C.L. McNeely (eds), *Encyclopedia of Big Data*. Living Edition. Springer. Available at: https://link.springer.com/referenceworkentry/10.1007%2F978-3-319-32001-4_44-1(accessed 18 March 2019).

Robinson, D. and Garratt, C. (2008) *Introducing Ethics: A Graphic Guide*. London: Icon Books.

Robson, G. and Olavarria, C.M. (2016) 'Big Collusion: Corporations, Consumers, and the Digital Surveillance State', in R.A. Cropf (ed.), *Ethical Issues and Citizen Rights in the Era of Digital Government Surveillance*. Hershey, PA: IGI Global, pp. 127–144.

Rodriguez, S. and Groom, N. (2018) 'Inside Tesla's Troubled New York Solar Factor', *Reuters*. Online edition, 8 August. Available at: https://www.reuters.com/article/us-tesla-solar-insight/inside-teslas-troubled-new-york-solar-factory-idUSKBN1KT0DU (accessed 8 February 2019).

Rogers, E. (2003 [1962]) *Diffusion of Innovations* (5th edn). New York: Free Press.

Rosner, H. (2018) 'The Absurdity of Trump Officials Eating at Mexican Restaurants During an Immigration Crisis', *The New Yorker*. Online edition, 22 June. Available at: https://www.newyorker.com/culture/annals-of-gastronomy/the-unsurprising-absurdity-of-kirstjen-nielsen-and-stephen-miller-eating-mexican-food-during-a-border-crisis (accessed 8 February 2019).

Rossiter, N. (2016) *Software, Infrastructure, Labor: A Media Theory of Logistical Nightmares*. New York: Routledge.

Rowland, W. (2006) *The Spirit of the Web*. Toronto: Thomas Allen.

Ruppel Shell, E. (2009) *Cheap: The High Cost of Discount Culture*. New York: Penguin.

Rusbult, C. and Martz, J.M. (1995) 'Remaining in an Abusive Relationship: An Investment Model Analysis of Nonvoluntary Dependence', *Personality and Social Psychology*, 21(6): 558–571.

Said, E. (1994) *Culture and Imperialism*. New York: Vintage.

Santa Clara County v. Southern Pacific Railroad Co. (1886) 118 U.S. 394.

Sartre, J. (2003 [1943]) *Being and Nothingness*. London: Routledge.

Sassatelli, R. (2007) *Consumer Culture: History, Theory and Politics*. London: Sage.

Saxena, S.B. (2014) *Made in Bangladesh, Cambodia, and Sri Lanka: The Labor Behind the Global Garments and Textiles Industries*. Amherst, NY: Cambria.

Scaraboto, D. and Fischer, E. (2013) 'Frustrated Fatshionistas: An Institutional Theory Perspective on the Quest for Greater Choice in Mainstream Markets', *Journal of Consumer Research*, 6 (April): 1234–1257.

Schau, H.J, Muñiz, Jr, A.M. and Arnould, E.J. (2009) 'How Brand Community Practices Create Value', *Journal of Marketing*, 73(5): 30–51.

Scholz, T. (2013) 'Why Does Digital Labor Matter Now?', in T. Scholz (ed.), *Digital Labor: The Internet as Playground and Factory*. New York: Routledge, 1–9.

Schumacher, E.F. (1973) *Small is Beautiful*. London: Blond & Briggs.

Schwartz, S.H. (1990) 'Individualism-Collectivism: Critique and Proposed Refinements', *Journal of Cross-Cultural Psychology*, 21(2): 139–157.

Scott, W.R. (2001) 'Introduction', in W.R. Scott and S. Christensen (eds), *The Institutional Construction of Organizations* 2nd (edn). London: Sage, pp. 95–111.

Settis, S. (2016) *If Venice Dies*. New York: New Vessel Press.

Shaw, E.H. and Jones, D.G.B. (2005) 'A History of Schools of Marketing Thought', *Marketing Theory*, 5(3): 239–281.

Skov, L. (2014) 'Fashion', in J. Smith Maguire and J. Matthews (eds), *The Cultural Intermediaries Reader*. London: Sage, pp. 113–124.

Slater, D. (1999) *Consumer Culture & Modernity*. Cambridge: Polity.

Smith, A. (1776) *The Wealth of Nations*. London: W. Strahan and T. Cadell.

Smith, A. (1757) *The Theory of Moral Sentiments*. Edinburgh: Andrew Millar.

Smith, D. (2006) *Globalization: The Hidden Agenda*. Cambridge: Polity.

Smythe, D.W. (1977) 'Communications: Blindspot of Western Marxism', *Canadian Journal of Political and Society Theory*, 1(3): 1–28.

Solomon, M.R., Bamossy, G.J., Søren, T.A. and Hogg, M.K. (2013) *Consumer Behaviour: A European Perspective*. Harlow: Pearson.

Sparks, J.R. and Hunt, S.D. (1998) 'Marketing Researcher Ethical Sensitivity: Conceptualization, Measurement, and Exploratory Investigation', *Journal of Marketing*, 62 (April): 92–109.

Stacey, E.B. (2018) *Global Diaspora Politics and Social Movements: Emerging Research and Opportunities*. Hershey, PA: IGI Global.

Steiner, R.L. (1976) 'The Prejudice Against Marketing', *Journal of Marketing*, 40(3): 2–9.

Stevenson, H. and Dryzek, J.S. (2014) *Democratizing Global Climate Governance*. Cambridge: Cambridge University Press.

Sunstein, C. (2018) *#republic*. Princeton, NJ: Princeton University Press.

Swedberg, R. (2003) *Principles of Economic Sociology*. Princeton, NJ: Princeton University Press.

Sylla, N. (2014) *The Fair Trade Scandal*. Athens, OH: Ohio University Press.

Tadajewski, M. (2006) 'Remembering Motivation Research: Toward an Alternative Genealogy of Interpretive Consumer Research', *Marketing Theory*, 6(4): 429–466.

The Telegraph (staff) (2008) 'Marks & Spencer: A Recent History', *Telegraph*. Online edition, 2 July. Available at: www.telegraph.co.uk/finance/newsbysector/retailandconsumer/2792584/Marks-and-Spencer-A-recent-history.html (accessed 8 February 2019).

Temin, P. and Vines, D. (2014) *Keynes: Useful Economics for the World Economy*. Cambridge, MA: MIT Press.

Toms, S. and Zhang, Q. (2016) 'Marks & Spencer and the Decline of the British Textile Industry, 1950–2000', *Business History Review*, 90(1): 3–30.

Tosh, J. (2009) *The Pursuit of History*. London: Routledge.

Tosh, J. (2008) *Why History Matters*. New York: Palgrave.

Turow, J. (2017) *The Aisles Have Eyes: How Retailers Track Your Shopping, Strip Your Privacy, and Define Your Power*. New Haven, CT: Yale University Press.

Twitchell, J.B. (1997) *Adcult USA: The Triumph of Advertising in American Culture*. New York: Columbia University Press.

Üstüner, T. and Holt, D.B. (2010) 'Toward a Theory of Status Consumption in Less Industrialized Countries', *Journal of Consumer Research*, 37(1): 37–56.

Usunier, J. and Lee, J.A. (2013) *Marketing Across Cultures*. Harlow: Pearson.

Vance, A. (2016) *Elon Musk: Tesla, SpaceX, and the Quest for a Fantastic Future*. London: Virgin Books.

Vanderheiden, S. (2009) *Atmospheric Justice: A Political Theory of Climate Change*. Oxford: Oxford University Press.

Walby, S. (2009) *Globalization & Inequalities*. London: Sage.

Wallerstein, I. (2004) *World Systems Analysis: An Introduction*. Durham, NC: Duke University Press.

Washington, H. and Cook, J. (2011) *Climate Change Denial: Heads in the Sand*. Abingdon: Earthscan.

Wilhide, E. (2016) *Scandinavian Home: A Comprehensive Guide to Mid-Century Modern Scandinavian Designers*. London: Quadrille Publishing.

Witoszek, N,, and A. Midttun (2018), 'Eco-Modernity Nordic Style: The Challenge of Aligning Ecological and Socio-Economic Sustainability', in N. Witoszek and A. Midttun (eds), *Sustainable Modernity: The Nordic Model and Beyond*. Abingdon: Routledge.

Wood, E.M. (2002) *The Origin of Capitalism: A Longer View*. London: Verso.

Zey, M. (1998) *Rational Choice Theory and Organizational Theory: A Critique*. London: Sage.

Žižek, S. (2009) *First As Tragedy, Then As Farce*. London: Verso.

Žižek, S. (2000) *The Ticklish Subject: The Absent Centre of Political Ontology*. London: Verso.

Index